THE GREEK ISLANDS
Genius Loci

View of Naxos island seen through the monumental doorway of the Archaic temple.
Thomas Hope (1769-1831)   Watercolour, 44 x 29 cm.   Benaki Museum, Inv. No. 27375.
© 2010 Benaki Museum, Athens.

Author's acknowledgements

This series of twenty books covering the Aegean Islands is the fruit of many years of solitary dedication to a job difficult to accomplish given the extent of the subject matter and the geography involved. My belief throughout has been that only what is seen with the eyes can trustfully be written about; and to that end I have attempted to walk, ride, drive, climb, sail and swim these Islands in order to inspect everything talked about here. There will be errors in this text inevitably for which, although working in good faith, I alone am responsible. Notwithstanding, I am confident that these are the best, most clearly explanatory and most comprehensive artistic accounts currently available of this vibrant and historically dense corner of the Mediterranean.

Professor Robin Barber, author of the last, general, *Blue Guide to Greece* (based in turn on Stuart Rossiter's masterful text of the 1960s), has been very generous with support and help; and I am also particularly indebted to Charles Arnold for meticulously researched factual data on the Islands and for his support throughout this project. I could not have asked for a more saintly and helpful editor, corrector and indexer than Judy Tither. Efi Stathopoulou, Peter Cocconi, Marc René de Montalembert, Valentina Ivancich, William Forrester and Geoffrey Cox have all given invaluable help; and I owe a large debt of gratitude to John and Jay Rendall for serial hospitality and encouragement. For companionship on many journeys, I would like to thank a number of dear friends: Graziella Seferiades, Ivan Tabares, Matthew Kidd, Martin Leon, my group of Louisianan friends, and my brother Iain— all of whose different reactions to and passions for Greece have been a constant inspiration.

This work is dedicated with admiration and deep affection to Ivan de Jesus Tabares-Valencia who, though a native of the distant Andes mountains, from the start understood the profound spiritual appeal of the Aegean world.

McGILCHRIST'S GREEK ISLANDS

5. THE SPORADES

GENIUS LOCI PUBLICATIONS
London

McGilchrist's Greek Islands The Sporades
First edition

Published by Genius Loci Publications
54 Eccleston Road, London W13 0RL

Nigel McGilchrist © 2010
Nigel McGilchrist has asserted his moral rights.

ISBN 978-1-907859-07-6

A CIP catalogue record of this book is available from the British Library.

The author and publisher cannot accept responsibility or liability for
information contained herein, this being in some cases difficult to verify
and subject to change.

Layout and copy-editing by Judy Tither

Cover design by Kate Buckle

Maps and plans by Nick Hill Design

Printed and bound in Great Britain by TJ International Ltd, Padstow, Cornwall

The island maps in this series are based on the cartography of
Terrain Maps
Karneadou 4, 106 75 Athens, Greece
T: +30 210 609 5759, Fx: +30 210 609 5859
terrain@terrainmaps.gr
www.terrainmaps.gr

This book is one of twenty which comprise the complete, detailed
manuscript which the author prepared for the *Blue Guide: Greece,
the Aegean Islands* (2010), and on which the *Blue Guide* was
based. Some of this text therefore appears in the *Blue Guide*.

CONTENTS

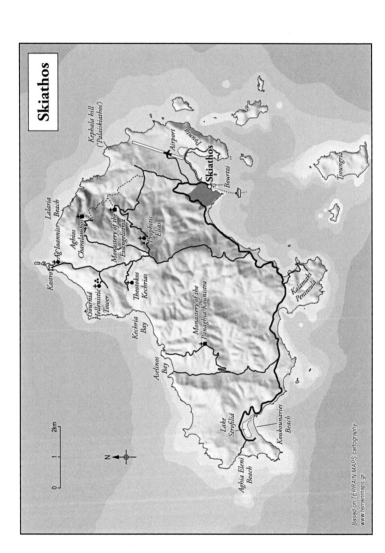

Skiathos

Kephala hill ('Palaiskiathos')

Lalaria
Beach

Ag. Ioannis

Aghios
Chatzelkynias

Kastro

Gournia

Hellenistic
Tower

Monastery of the
Evangelistria

Prophitis
Elias

Theotokos
Kechrias

Kechria
Bay

Airport

Skiathos

Bourtzi

Troulia

Tsougria

Kalamaki
Peninsula

Monastery of the
Panaghia Kounistra

Aselinos
Bay

Lake
Stroflia

Koukounaries
Beach

Aghia Eleni
Beach

0   1   2km

N

Based on TERRAIN MAPS cartography
www.terrainmaps.gr

SKIATHOS

The name 'Skiá-' (shadow) '-athos' (Mount Athos) is believed to refer to the fact that, at the time of the summer solstice, the shadow cast by the rising sun from the pinnacle of Mount Athos, 130km (80 miles) to the northeast, is said to touch the island of Skiathos. (The 14th century traveller, Sir John Mandeville, claimed something very similar of the same mountain, when he said its shadow at sunset reached the isle of Lemnos '76 miles away': but he was later to be censured as the 'greatest liar of all time' by Sir Thomas Browne.)

Skiathos is famous above all for its dense pine woods and its magnificent sandy beaches. This fame has brought the island prosperity and employment in the shape of an ever enlarging tourism industry, which in turn has done much to transform the appearance and the tranquillity of the town and of the island's south coast. In effect, this is a thin corridor of intense development, and the sparsely inhabited and densely wooded north of the island has been affected by it hardly at all. Some of the prettiest and most untouched bays in the Sporades can still be found on the north side of the island, and there are abundant walks to be made in the peace and shade of the hills in the interior. Although Skiathos is primarily a destination for recreation more than for visits of cultural interest, a stay on the island can happily combine both nonetheless. The deserted Byzantine settlement of Kastro, on a pinnacle of rock overlooking the sea at the northernmost point of the island, is a magnificent and dramatic site, which alone justifies a journey to the island. Inland of Kastro, is the ruined Hellenistic tower at Gourniá. There is the monastery of the Evangelistria, which is of interest both for its fine *catholicon* and for its historical associations; the painted church of the Panaghia Kounistra, in the south of the island; as well as many other chapels and peaceful hermitages in the hills of the interior. In addition to the celebrated beaches of the island are the less visited ones which are often of greater beauty: Aghia Eleni in the west and—more difficult of access—the bays of Kechriá and Ligariés, to the north.

The spare and self-sufficient simplicity of the Skiathos that Alexander Papadiamantis evoked with poignancy and unsentimentality in his writings at the turn of the last century, is now long gone from the island today, but the small uncluttered house where he lived and died in the centre of the town, is a moving window onto that world which no longer exists. It provides a pointed contrast to the swirling culture of materialism which pervades the town today.

HISTORY AND LEGEND

Settlers allegedly from Caria, followed later by Thessal-
ians, were the first stable inhabitants of the island. In the
7th century BC colonists from Chalcis in Euboea arrived
and later founded a coastal settlement on the Kephala peninsula in the northeast corner of the island, known as
'*Palaiskiathos*'. In Classical times a second city succeeded
it, with a new site on the low hill in the south west of modern Skiathos town, which controlled the bay and its dou-
ble-port. Sections of the 4th century enceinte of walls are
all that remain of this city. Skiathos played its part during
the Second Persian War providing solid Greek support at a
geographically strategic point on the enemy's route south,
and relaying vital information signals. In the waters off the
island, three Greek guardships of the fleet at Artemision
were surprised by a squadron of Xerxes's fleet (providing
Herodotus with one of his most realistic details—the capture of the wounded captain, Pytheas of Aegina, who was
spared for his valour and later rescued at Salamis. *Hist*.
VII, 181). At the same time, three ships of the Persian ad-
vance-guard ran aground on a reef, which Herodotus calls
'the Ant', between Skiathos and the mainland of Magnesia, which the Persians subsequently marked with a stone

beacon. Skiathos joined the Delian League after the war (paying a tribute of 1,000 drachmas) and became in effect a subject ally of Athens. After the Battle of Chaeronea in 338 bc, the island passed under Macedonian rule and was later devastated by Philip V of Macedon in 220 BC. Freed by Rome in 197 BC, it was gifted to Athens by Mark Anthony in acknowledgement of her help after the Battle of Philippi in 42 BC.

In Byzantine times, Skiathos belonged to the *theme* of Macedonia. In 1204, after the Fourth Crusade, the island came under the possession of the Ghisi family together with the other Sporades islands. In 1276 they were driven out by the Byzantine fleet. After the fall of Constantinople in 1453, the inhabitants sought the protection of the Venetian Republic, which governed the island until it was captured for the Turks by Khaireddin Barbarossa in 1538. Skiathos subsequently was all but deserted: habitation hesitantly returned to Kastro in the 17th century, but then later transferred to the site of the ancient town only in the relative security of the 19th century. The island became part of the newly formed Greek State in 1830. Skiathos was the home of the novelists Alexander Papadiamantis and Alexander Moraitidis in the late 19th and early 20th centuries.

During the Second World War, Skiathos was a crucial place of refuge for retreating Allied troops (New Zealanders in the majority) who had been cut off by the German advance through Greece. Many sought safety at Kastro while waiting for boats to take them to Turkey. Later the town of Skiathos suffered a torching by retreating German troops: hence the prevailing modernity of its architecture.

The guide to the island has been divided into two sections:-
*   *Skiathos Chora*
*   *Around the island*

SKIATHOS CHORA

The pine-clad rocky promontory of **Bourtzi**, which juts
out into the bay in front of Skiathos Chora, today divides
the port into two: to the north is the featureless modern
port where the ferries dock, and to the west is the more
attractive old port, which is used for fishing boats and
other small craft. In Antiquity the promontory would
have been an island; it still was at the time that the Ghisi
brothers established their dominion over the island in the
early 13th century by building a fortress here. The rise is
now crowned by a neoclassical building—slightly out of
proportion to its site—which was formerly a *Gymnasion*
or high school, and today is used as a 'Cultural Centre'. A
peacefulness pervades the minute headland and its café
is a pleasant place to sit. On the grassy slope above the
causeway there are a few ancient stones, a couple of which,
unusually, still possess their bronze clamps *in situ*. Bourtzi is sometimes referred to in older writings as the 'Castle
of Aghios Giorgios': the church to St George, which once
occupied this site, is now gone, but these pieces of antiquity may have been amongst the stones brought from the
ancient town and incorporated in the church's structure
when it was built. Beside the causeway are monuments to

Papadiamantis and Moraitidis, the island's most famous men of letters (*see below*).

The **Chora** spreads over two hills: one, to the north, is crowned by the church of Aghios Nikolaos with a windmill at its summit; the other, to the south, occupies the site of the ancient acropolis. The town's main street, Odos Papadiamantis, winds through the valley in between, across the area where the ancient *agorá* would have been. Visible evidence of the ancient town is almost non-existent beyond a few miscellaneous pieces—capitals, columns, and dedicatory inscriptions of late date—which have been gathered in the forecourt of the *Demarcheion*, or Town Hall.

A little inland and above the western end of the old port, is the town's 19th century cathedral, dedicated to the **Tris Gerarches**—SS. Basil, John Chrysostom and Gregory the Theologian. The area beyond the cathedral to the west is a web of narrow streets with very much more the feel of an island 'chora'; these lead uphill to the church of the **Panaghia Limniá** at the summit (also 19th century). In front of its east end is an impressive example of a **Skiathos mansion**: the house has a fine balcony with columns on the upper level and gives a sense of the simple grandeur of the dwellings of the rich trading and ship-building families on the island in the last century.

The building is currently awaiting restoration after a fire. Further north from here is the church of Aghia Triada; between it and the cemetery is the hill of the ancient acropolis, of which there are only scattered remains—no more than a few single marble pieces scattered in the area of pine trees just above the cemetery and on the edge of the car-park below. To the west a once fortified escarpment drops to the sea.

In the centre of the town behind the new port, and on the corner of a small *plateia* just a few steps east of the main shopping thoroughfare, the **house of Alexander Papadiamantis**, who through his writings has made his native island famous beyond its shores, has been preserved. (*Open daily 9.30–1 & 5–8; closed Mon.*) The humble simplicity of this house is a reflection of the almost monastic soul of the writer who lived here, as well as of the more general simplicity of life on the Greek islands 100 years ago. The room where he died in 1911 has been preserved unchanged, and the house contains just a few of the objects relating to his last sojourn here. This is the house of a man who hated noise and ostentation of every kind: one is left wondering what he would make of the Skiathos of today.

ALEXANDROS PAPADIAMANTIS

Papadiamantis was born on Skiathos in March 1851 into a family predominantly of clergymen and sailors; he was educated first on the island, and latterly in Chalcis and in Athens. Aged 21 he visited Mount Athos—a defining moment of his youth which reinforced his natural religious bent. He read philosophy at university and worked for the Greek press as a translator and story writer. In his life he published nearly 20 novels and over 100 short stories. In 1908 he returned to his native Skiathos, and died there in January 1911 at the age of 60. His writing has something of that astringent quality which characterises every aspect of Greek island life: no words are ever wasted, and what is not said is often just as significant as what is said. The scenes he describes and settings he chooses are inhabited by simple folk and simple, but intense, joys: his vision, however, is that of the unsentimental realist, and his conclusions are fundamentally melancholy. He exalted the Greek landscape, the dignified simplicity of its people, and their ancient traditions: what Jean François Millet did for French rural life in his paintings, Papadia-

mantis did for Greek rural life in his writings. Millet
was sometimes criticised for what were considered
the repetitive and often inconsequential subjects of
his drawings and paintings, and a similar commen-
tary has been levelled against Papadiamantis. Some
of his stories can have little objective activity, but
their virtue lies in the deep tranquillity they convey,
and in the empathetic and unsentimental eye that
the author turns upon a world which he sensed, at
every turn, was slipping away. He wrote in a simple,
poetic Greek and exalted the poetry of simple lives.
He never lost his deep moral conviction and devout
religious passion; the house where he lived is of a
monastic simplicity which matches the spareness of
his choice of words.

The Papadiamantis Museum has a small shop
where it is possible to find his works both in Greek
and in translation. An off-print is available in Greek
and in English, of his hard and jewel-like short story,
Love in the Snow.

The northern extremity of the harbour of Skiathos ends
in a shallow lagoon defined by a narrow spit of land
which cuts across to the hilly promontory of Pounta to

the east. This was once the centre of the island's most important and vital industry—boat-building. The tide of that industry has withdrawn and left the **boatyards** somewhat stranded, although in recent years the demand for traditional wooden caïques is reviving. The manufacture of boats was underpinned by the plentiful supply of pine-wood from the hills of the island. Today the level of activity is diminished, but it is fascinating nonetheless to see the shaped wooden elements being prepared and seasoned, the craft slowly taking form, and the visible presence of a highly specialized skill which has its roots in a long history.

AROUND THE ISLAND

NORTH OF CHORA

(*Chora = 0.0km for distances in text*)

The coastal road out of the eastern end of the Chora heads towards the Pounda peninsula: after 1km, before the boatyards, a left branch circles anticlockwise around the airport compound. At the opposite (northern) end of the runway is the peninsula hill of **Képhala** (3.5km:

marked on some maps as Cape Katergáki), which projects into the sea towards the northeast; remains of buildings and the ruins of a rubble-masonry enceinte of walls here bear witness to the fact that this promontory was the site of the island's first settlement, '**Palaiskiathos**', founded probably in late Geometric times (8th century BC). Evidence of the town's necropolis of the Classical period has come to light behind the shallow bay to the west of the promontory. Palaiskiathos was abandoned in the 4th century BC in favour of the new city of Skiathos on the site of today's Chora.

The principal road to the north of the island also leaves from the eastern end of Chora, heads inland and turns off the town's ring-road to the right towards Kalývia, 200m after the junction for the airport terminal. At a subsequent junction (2.3km), it heads west towards the hills and to the **monastery of the Evangelistria**. (5km. *Open 8–12 & 4–8.*) The setting is peaceful and wooded. The exterior of the monastery is a dignified stone construction dating from the end of the 18th century. A cross, in tiles, over the main entrance door bears the insignia 'ΙΣ/ΧΡ ΝΙ/ΚΑ' ('May the Victory be Jesus Christ's'). The compact courtyard inside is dominated by the pleasing alternation of sharply defined geometric forms in the domes and semidomes of the roof of the *catholicon*: this structure predates the buildings which surround it by as much as 250 years, although it must have been considerably restored and perhaps re-roofed between 1796 and 1806 when the monastery buildings were re-erected around it. Inside, the cupola is spacious, and the whole interior is unusually light. This striking effect is in part due to the lack of plaster rendering, which leaves the superb masonry-work visible in the half-domes and the cupola. Wall paintings of the 18th century, now much blackened, remain only behind the iconostasis and in the apse. There are delightful 19th century Italian tiles on the floor. The monastery buildings house a small museum of ecclesiastical artefacts and a library, and there is a spacious refectory on the south side.

In spite of the remote setting, the monastery found itself momentarily at the centre of Greek history in 1807 whilst giving refuge to independence fighters during the last years of Ottoman rule. A **Greek flag** (on display)—at this point, an early version just consisting of a white cross on a blue background—was made and raised here for the first time in the presence of Theodore Kolokotronis, Andreas Miaoulis and other leaders of the national revolt. They were sworn to the flag by the local bishop. The cross and tiny inscription over the monastery's main door now acquired a new significance.

A path beyond the Evangelistria monastery leads (45 minutes) to the isolated hermitage of **Aghios Charálambos** on the slopes of the island's highest mountain, to which the novelist Alexander Moraitidis (1850–1929), a relative and almost exact contemporary of Papadiamantis, retired shortly before his death. (*This can also be reached from here by unmade road from the junction beyond the spring of Prophitis Elias on the road to Kastro.*)

Five hundred metres before the end of the asphalt road at the Evangelistria Monastery, an unmade road leads off to the west by the church of the Zoödochos Pigi (4.2km). Following this, after 2km, there is a spring beneath large plane trees close by the church of Prophitis Elias, and a *taverna* with panoramic **views** of the south of the island. At a junction 300m beyond there are two consecutive right turns: the first leads only to Aghios Charalambos; the second, just beyond, should be taken to reach Kastro. This second road begins to descend and affords the possibility of three visits:

• after 700m (7.2km) there is a first left branch into the valley of Kechriá and to the 18th century church of **Panaghia Kechriás**. Only the *catholicon* survives from the monastery whose buildings have since perished; it is decorated with late Byzantine paintings in the interior. The track soon ends and a foot-path leads down beyond to the tranquil bays and beaches of **Kechriá** and **Ligariés**;

• after 1800m (8.3km) a second left branch leads west into the Gourniá area. Two hundred and fifty metres down this road is the church of Aghia Anastasia to the right-hand side amidst some trees; beside it is the massive base of a circular **Hellenistic watch-tower**. The curved limestone blocks from which it is made are meticulously cut and shaped, and their surface dressed by point and chisel. A reference in Herodotus (*Hist.* VII, 183), when he is telling of the capture by the Persians of two Greek guard ships in August 480 BC, mentions that 'news of what had happened was flashed to the Greeks at Artemision by fire-signal from Skiathos'. The sight-lines of this tower are towards the mainland of Magnesia rather than towards the north of Euboea and it must have been built at least 150 years later, in the mid 4th century BC: but it is nonetheless a visible, surviving element from a whole network of communications points which had already existed on these islands for some time;

- continuing north and passing the church of the Koimisis tis Theotokou, the road ends (9.7km) just above the promontory of Kastro. In the trees to the right is the church of **Aghios Ioannis**: just to its west is a long low ossuary—or rather a construction (possibly once a fountain head) being used as an ossuary. The decorative marble plaque on its front with a 'fount-of-life' motif gives no intimation that the interior is heaped with skulls and bones.

***Kastro** (10km)—one of the most remarkable sites in the Sporades—is best visited in the evening, when it is often empty and the dramatic beauty of its position is best appreciated. When it first comes into view, it is the audacity of the site that amazes. Equally audacious would be anyone who dared attempt to capture it, but the indefatigable Khaireddin Barbarossa laid siege to Kastro in 1538, and left it desolate and abandoned.

At exactly what point this rocky peninsula was first inhabited is not yet clear. The site was not unknown to the Ancients: there are some rock-cut steps and a platform in the cliff, low-down on the western side near to the sea. In the 13th century Geremia Ghisi may have established his principal fortress at Kastro, as the site of the ancient settlement on the south coast had become increasingly subject to pirate raids. When the island was slowly repopulated in the century after Barbarossa's attack, this became its only inhabited centre, and it was only after 1829 that Skiathos town grew up once again on the site of the ancient city. Even in its abandoned state today, Kastro gives a clear idea of a mediaeval acropolis, untouched and unaltered by later generations.

The **gate** is still well-preserved with the site of its drawbridge below; some antique elements of white marble have been incorporated into its lintels. The enceinte of walls is visible at several points, in particular up the west side of the promontory to the south of the drawbridge. At the northern extremity it drops down low and runs around the headland. The promontory was only the fortress, or 'acropolis', of the town; the settlement itself stretched all along the bay to the east, where there appear to have been churches on virtually every rocky eminence—some have walls that remain, some are visible only in plan, others are just rubble. The town also extended to the south at least as far as the church of Aghios Demetrios (whose foundations are visible just below where the modern road ends) and maybe even as far back as the spring at Aghios Ioannis. At its height this was a large settlement and it would have been natural to include such a source of water within the walls if possible.

Inside the citadel the problem of water had to be resolved in a different manner: immediately on passing through the entrance gate, there is a well-preserved cistern and fountain to the left. Within the citadel area, only the churches survive—as at the Palaiochora settlements on Kythera and on Aegina; all the houses (except for one which has been restored) have gone. The churches are of an architecturally simple design, namely a single-aisled hall with pitched roof. Only one of them, visible immediately ahead and to the right on entering, differs significantly, having a dome over the whole of its small, square plan. This was used as a mosque during the years of the Turkish Occupation, though it may well have been built as a church originally. Most of the churches have little decorative interest, except for that of **Christós sto Kástro** in the dip of the saddle. This is an early 16th century church which must have suffered destruction at the hands of Barbarossa. Its extensive wall-paintings of the life of Christ are of the 18th century: the wooden iconostasis is of the same date.

The site had obvious defensive appeal, but a number of problems remained—the lack of a protected harbour or anchorage; the difficult supply of water, in particular to the citadel; and the site's exposure to the often relentless north wind. The fact that, in spite of these difficulties, this was the island's principal settlement for many centuries in modern history is testimony to the fear and the siege-mentality that prevailed for so long amongst the island communities of the Aegean in the face of piracy.

SOUTH OF CHORA

To the south of Chora, the main road runs along the coast and passes successive sandy beaches which are pro-tected from the north wind, but have little atmosphere because of the proximity of buildings and of traffic. The road never really emerges from an area of unrelenting conurbation. The tracks that deviate towards the right, by contrast, soon climb deep into the forested valleys of the interior. Just before Troulos (7km) a metalled road heads to the right (north) for the bay of **Asélinos** and the **monastery of the Panaghia Kounístra** (11km. *Open 8.30–12.30 and 4–7.30*). After the busy activity of the coastal strip, this oasis is a joy to find—isolated on a green hillside, looking north towards Mount Pelion. The date of 1798 over the main door must refer to the building of the narthex only because the *catholicon* dates from the 15th century or earlier. Lying near to the entrance there are early Byzantine marble fragments which would suggest that there was a much older foundation here before. The church has a simple dome-on-cross form. The interesting **wall-paintings**, which cover nearly all the interior surfaces, are severely blackened with candle soot, except in the cupola where they have suffered the worse (and irreversible) fate of being drastically over-cleaned at some point in their history: this has upset the chromatic balance of the *Pantocrator* and the *Panoply of Heaven*. On the walls, it can be seen that the halos of the saints are made in an unusual fashion for wall-paintings, namely in silver/tin alloy which has been adhered to the surface of the wall. A breach in the plaster, just to the north of the door of entry, shows just how thin the plaster is, and how humbly it has been prepared, with straw to bind it. The 17th century iconostasis of carved wood displays two beautiful icons: the *Presentation of the Virgin*, and *Christ Enthroned*. The monastery now has one resident nun.

Three kilometres west along the main road beyond the junction at Troulos, is one of Greece's most famous beaches—the pine-bordered strand of **Koukounariés** (10km), which extends in a gentle sweep to the west, with a landlocked lagoon behind it. The area of the beach is now the object of strenuous conservation and protection. Fewer crowds and a beautiful open view across to Cape Artemision on the north of Euboea, is provided by the smaller, sandy beach of **Aghia Eleni** (11.5km) to the west, from where it is possible to contemplate, towards the left of the field of vision, the open arena of sea in which the Battle of Cape Artemision between the Greek and Persian fleets took place in August of 480 BC. Herodotus VII, 175–195 & VIII, 1–18, is the appropriate beach reading-material here. The southwestern point of the island at Pounda is the site of an ancient watch-tower, perhaps the successor to the signalling station mentioned by Herodotus.

PRACTICAL INFORMATION

370 02 Skiathos: area 47sq. km; perimeter 48km; resident population 5788; max. altitude 433 m. **Port Authority:** T. 24270 22017. **Travel information:** GATS Travel (T. 24270 24226, fax 24228; www.skiathos.gr)

ACCESS

Access to the island is easy both by boat and by air.
By air. Olympic Air currently operates a 50 minute, non-stop scheduled daily service to and from Athens. Charter companies fly direct to Skiathos from all over northern Europe in the summer months. The airport is 2km north of Chora.
By boat. The usual mainland port of departure is Volos, from which there are several daily services to Skiathos by fast car ferry and by hydrofoil. There are also less frequent connections (5 times weekly) to the mainland closer to Athens at Aghios Kostantinos, and to Kymi on Euboea. Skiathos is on the boat route to Skopelos and Alonnisos, and all the services which call at Skiathos also communicate with these islands.

LODGING

There is a huge choice of hotels on the island. Sophisticated and elegant designer luxury can be had at the **Aegean Suites Hotel**, 1km west of the main town at Megali Ammos (*T. 24270 24069; fax. 24070, www. aegeansuites.com*); alternatively, central and economical lodgings can be found on the front in Skiathos at the **Hotel Meltemi** (*T. 24270 22493*). Many visitors may simply be in search of somewhere away from the noise of Skiathos town at night: on the peninsula of Pounta, east of the town, at a distance of less than 2km from the centre, is the **Hotel Emy** (*T. 24270 24119; fax. 24118*) in the peace and quiet of its own garden.

EATING

Of the many good places to eat on Skiathos, a particular favourite with locals and visitors alike is **Agnadio,** on the road past the airport, on the way to the Evangelistria monastery. Set away from the bustle of the waterfront on Odos Kapodistrias, between the two large churches of the Tris Gerarches and the Panaghia Limniá, is the **Taverna Alexandros**. It provides good quality, traditional Greek food in a small square, protected from the wind.

FURTHER READING

A good selection of short stories set in Skiathos by Alexandros Papadiamantis (translated into English by Elizabeth Konstantinides) has been published as *Tales from a Greek Island*, Johns Hopkins University Press, 1987. Another masterfully translated collection of his stories is the volume, *The Boundless Garden*, published by Denise Harvey, Limni, Evvia. One of Papadiamantis's most powerful and celebrated works is the novella *The Murderess* which has been sensitively translated by the poet, Peter Levi, S.J.

SKOPELOS

In the last half-hour of the boat journey to Skopelos from the mainland, the ferry rounds Cape Gourouni and sails parallel to the eastern shore of the island, past bay after bay of steeply sloping pine forests and rushing streams. Scarcely a track or a dwelling is visible. A cliff-top chapel perhaps is glimpsed, then nothing again—just dense green slopes and the astringent scent of pine and of the sea. From the viewpoint of our city-centric culture, we have traditionally seen the islands as remote and peripheral, as places of retreat. Indeed their isolation is what gives us pleasure. But, in historical terms, we see things inside out: in prehistory and Antiquity, it was the sea that connected, facilitated and brought communities into life-giving contact with one another, and it was the land-mass of the mainland that was peripheral. This deserted and beautiful coastline was a busy thoroughfare of Antiquity; tiny craft with obsidian and minerals from Milos in the 3rd millennium BC, Minoan metal traders in the 2nd millennium, and in the first millennium BC barges laden with amphorae containing the island's prized wine, destined for the Black Sea, all plied up and down this same coast. And what we see of it today has changed little over 5,000 years from what was seen of it then by those early voyagers.

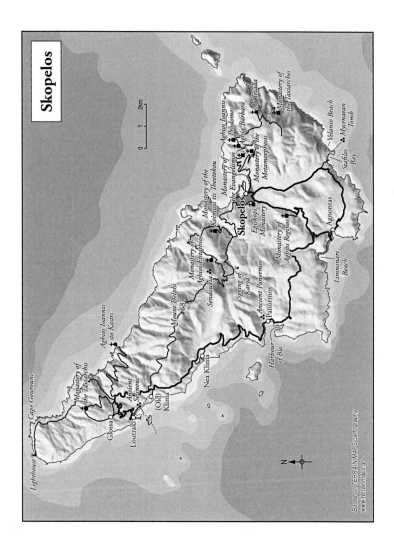

It is remarkable how well-preserved Skopelos is at the beginning of the 3rd millennium AD; it seems to have found a just balance between the busy normality of its Chora, a contained amount of tourism, and the preservation of its large areas of mountainous forest and coastline. Skopelos has the greatest depth of all the Northern Sporades islands—a richness of architecture which Alonnisos lacks, a clear identity and self-sufficiency which Skiathos has surrendered to tourism, and an economic importance and commercial vitality which have passed Skyros by. There is the appealing wooded coastline with coves and beaches down the west side of the island, and deep forest valleys in the interior. The town has an attractive and varied domestic architecture and an unparalleled number of interesting churches with paintings and fine wood-carving. In the hills to the south, east and west of the Chora are over a dozen monasteries, dating from the late Middle Ages to the 18th century—amongst which, the remote and tranquil hermitage-monastery of the Taxiarches. Of the island's vitality in Antiquity, and its three cities of *Peparethos*, *Pánormos* and *Selinoús*, the visible remains are scant, but there is an enigmatic site high on the slopes of Mount Delfi at 'Sendoukia', where a small and curious necropolis occupies one of the most magnificent positions in all of the Northern Aegean.

HISTORY AND LEGEND

The discovery of a substantial Bronze Age shaft-grave on the promontory at Stafilos in 1936 provided clear evidence of Cretan colonisation on the island in the late 17th century BC. Dubbed locally the 'tomb of King Staphylos', because of the rich grave gifts which were unearthed in it, the find gave tendentious credence to the legend that the island's first notable ruler was Staphylos, the son of Ariadne. As to whether he was her son by the hero Theseus or by the god Dionysos the sources are characteristically ambiguous, as Plutarch points out (*Theseus*, 21). His brother was Pepárethos, the name which the city and island of Skopelos bore all through Antiquity. Since '*stafili*' is the ancient Greek for a 'grape bunch', and the name Pepárethos could be seen as cognate with the verb '*pepainein*', 'to ripen', we may simply be looking at the mythical explanation of the island's importance and fame throughout ancient times as a producer of a highly prized wine—the '*Πεπαρήθιος οἶνος*' which was exported to points all around the Euxine (Black) Sea, as the presence of the island's amphorae there show. In historical times, much of the island's history is identical with Skiathos: the city of *Peparethos* (modern Skopelos Chora) was founded in the 7th century BC, by colonists from Chalcis in Euboea, along with two other cities on the island—*Pánormos* and *Selinoús* (modern-day Loutráki). Some remains of the acropolis walls of all three cities are still visible. Skopelos joined the Delian League, paying the substantial annual tribute of 3 talents, indicative of its relative prosperity and trading strength, based on the export of its wine. In 427 BC earthquakes and tidal waves damaged the city of Peparethos according to Thucydides (III, 89). After the Battle of Chaeronea in 338 BC, the island passed under Macedonian rule: it was freed by Rome in 197 bc, but was later gifted by Mark Anthony after the Battle of Philippi in 42 BC to Athens in acknowledgement of the city's support.

Christianity came to the island most notably in the person of the bishop-saint, Reginos, who was martyred for his faith under Julian the Apostate in 362 or 363 AD. In the 6th century the island's name first emerges as 'Schepola' in Byzantine chronicles. Together with Skiathos, Skopelos belonged to the Byzantine *theme* of Macedonia. In 1204, after the Fourth Crusade, it came under the possession of the Ghisi family. In 1276 they were driven out by the Byzantine fleet. After the fall of Constantinople in 1453 the inhabitants sought the protection of the Venetian Republic, which governed Skopelos until it was captured for the Turks by Khaireddin Barbarossa in 1538, who—as was his generally his custom—left the island devastated and depopulated. Under Turkish control, however, the islanders possessed a number of privileges and freedoms. During the 1820s Skopelos accepted refugees from Thessaly and Macedonia, and in the 1920s, from Asia Minor. The island became part of the new Greek state in 1830.

The guide to the island has been divided into three sections.
* *Skopelos Chora*
* *The south and east of the island*
* *The north of the island*

SKOPELOS CHORA

THE KASTRO AND OLD HARBOUR AREA

From the sea, the ascending sweep of the *Chora of Sko-pelos** is an amphitheatre of clear and simple architectural forms—triangles, squares and cylinders—enhanced by contrasts in the building materials: the irregular, silvery shapes of the schist roof-tiles, the thin wooden balconies and the smooth, uniformly whitewashed walls. The roof-scape is constantly broken by the towers and cupolas of churches. There are a great many churches—allegedly 123 in the Chora alone (though the true number is more like a half of that). It is a reflection of the unbroken prosperity of Skopelos and of its relative freedom under the period of Turkish domination that these highly individual churches are decorated with wall-paintings, fine iconostases, architectural details, and in some cases with Ottoman ceramics.

*An itinerary follows which covers the oldest quarter of the town: it begins at the northern end of the port, climbs up to the Kastro, and re-descends to the front again not far from the striking building of the **Demarcheion** (Town Hall) which stands at the centre of the water front.*

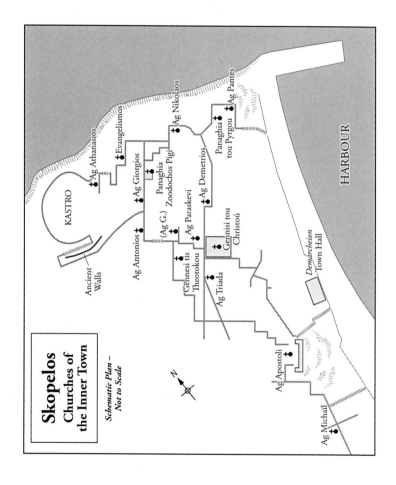

Skopelos
Churches of
the Inner Town

Schematic Plan –
Not to Scale

KASTRO

Ancient
Walls

Ag Athanasios

Evangelismos

Ag Giorgios

Panaghia
Zoodochos Pigi

Ag Nikolaos

Ag Pantes

Panaghia
tou Pyrgou

Ag Demetrios

Ag Antonios

Panaghia
(Ag G.)

Ag Paraskevi

Gennisi tis
Theotokou

Gennisi tou
Christoú

Ag Triada

Demárcheion
Town Hall

HARBOUR

Ag Apostoli

Ag Michaíl

Climbing up

The northern end of the promenade is closed and anchored by the long, low mass of the church of the **Panaghia tou Pyrgou** sitting on the rocks above. Its name ('Virgin of the Tower') would suggest that this point of the promontory was once marked by a watch-tower. The old part of the church—the domed, inscribed-cross core of the building—is 15th century, with a spacious narthex and elegant bell tower added in the 19th century. There are remains of wall-paintings near the south door. Immediately to seaward of it stands the tiny chapel of **Aghii Pantes** (All Saints): there is rare (for Skopelos) tile-work in the construction of its eastern apse, unobtrusive vine-decorations around the door, and a small ogival niche to the left of the entrance, for the placing of an icon on feast days.

Higher up above these two churches, and to the left of the path, is **Aghios Nikolaos**—another small church of inscribed cross-with-dome plan which has had a vestibule added to its north side: the section of an ancient column, with dowel-hole in its centre, is prominently displayed on the exterior of the east end. A further climb (keeping to the edge of the hill) brings you to a terrace with the seats of a café from which the whole cascade of architectural volumes below can be appreciated. Slightly set back from here, is the 15th century church of the **Evangelismós** (the Annunciation), which is entered through an enclosed courtyard to the south. The church has satisfying proportions both inside and out. The repainting of the apse is regrettable but does not detract from the beauty of the 16th and 17th century **icons** on the screen. The characteristic variety of colour and shape in the 'fish-scale' schist roof, and the church's pleasing octagonal drum are best appreciated from the stairs above and behind. These steps lead up to a higher level and the church of **Aghios Athanasios tou Kastrou** which is of the 11th century and probably the oldest church in Chora. Its design is a simple barrel vaulted nave, which has been substantially buttressed on its south side. The lateral wall-paintings of figures of saints, however, are of 500 years later, and the carved iconostasis is of the 18th century. The church's size and its proximity to the old citadel/acropolis would suggest that it had particular importance early on, and may have been the original episcopal church of the island. From Aghios Athanasios, it is a short climb to the summit where a taverna unexpectedly occupies the site of the **fortress castle** built by Filippo Ghisi in the 13th century. The area of the castle is small, and probably represents the keep of a larger fortified complex which extended to the north and west. Descending the steps at the rear (west side) and

looking back, the base of the large masonry blocks of the
walls of the ancient acropolis of *Peparethos* are visible at
the lower level. These are of the 5th century BC and func-
tion as the solid foundations for the mediaeval walls built
on top of them. Other vestiges of ancient retaining walls
can be glimpsed higher up on the hillside which lies to
the west and northwest of the fortress: these created the
terraces on which the temples of Athena and Dionysos
originally stood, commanding magnificent views and visible from far out to sea.

Descending

Taking the narrow street which skirts closely around the
south side of the bottom of the castle and descends a narrow alley between houses anti-clockwise round the hill,
you will come to the end of the path at some steps and
to an alley which runs transversely. To the right of you is
the church of Aghios Antonios and to the left is **Aghios
Giorgios**, clearly recognisable by its cupola, with a tall
drum decorated with blind arcades: it vies with Aghios
Athanasios (*see above*) as one of the oldest churches in
Chora, but it is a more intimate space and more beautiful building, with a domed Greek-cross plan. The interior
has a beautiful pebble floor: there are wall paintings on
the west wall which, though venerable, are in poor condi-

tion. Further along the same street on the opposite side, through a gate and with a small space or *avli* in front of it, is another remarkable church, dedicated to the **Panaghia** (**Zoödochos Pigi**). This has fine paintings in the apse and sanctuary: a *Christ and Virgin* blessing above a ring of saints; and a *Lamentation* scene, to the left.

By returning back past Aghios Giorgios and Aghios Antonios at the end of the street, you come to steps which lead down towards an imposing low-lying church; as you approach, the conical rises and striking silhouette of its schist-tiled roof appear before you like a relief map of an island landscape. This is the church of the *****Génnisi tou Christoú** (Nativity of Christ)—architecturally satisfying and highly unusual both inside and out.

The core of the church dates from the late 15th century, but a broad parallel nave, or *parecclesion*, has been added on the north side in the 19th century; on the south, the addition of the long low **arcaded porch**, which forms one side of an en-closed courtyard, is a particularly beautiful feature, typical of the architecture of churches in northern Greece. The in-terior space of the church is dominated by a heterogeneous **group of eight columns**: two monolithic columns with early Byzantine capitals, two with undecorated capitals, and four extraordinary columns composed of drums at the west end.

The floor incorporates an interesting orange/pink variety of stone, similar to *portasanta* marble from Chios: in fact it is native to the island and comes from the area of the promontory at Stafilos, where almost identical material can be seen in its natural state.

In the area of the Christoú are a number of smaller churches worthy of mention. Returning to the main street or alley above its west end and the bell tower, the small chapel of Aghia Paraskeví is directly opposite; to right (north) is the 12th century church of **Aghios Demetrios** (20m on the left), with wall-paintings of later date inside; to left is **Aghia Triada**. Straight uphill past Aghia Paraskeví and along the first alley to the left is a simple vaulted chapel, probably of the 16th century, dedicated to the **Génnisi tis Theotokou** (the Nativity of the Virgin), sitting below the level of the path to the left after about 25m. Its principal interest lies in its wooden *iconostasis, which must have been created for the church about a century later. The screen is carved perhaps with more vitality than subtlety, and is gilded and painted: but it incorporates a fine series of 16th century tempera panels, depicting scenes from the lives of Christ and of the Virgin, which run along the top, each framed with a scallop shell fan above within an arch. The doors of the screen are also painted. This is a rare piece for its un-restored, original condition and the quality of its painting. The church has a couple of ancient fragments and part of a fluted column in the forecourt by the entrance door.

By returning once again to the Christoú church and taking the path that goes downhill beside its arcaded south side, after five or six twists in the descent, you emerge at a church with a small shaded terrace to its south side and a pleasant view overlooking the port. This is the 11th century church of the A**ghii Apostoli**: its size, its single-aisle design, and its age are all similar to the church of Aghios Athanasios tou Kastrou (*above*). Inside are wall paintings of the 17th century: a fine row of saints along the south wall, with elaborate and richly painted robes. The plainness of the exterior of the east end which faces over the harbour is relieved by the inclusion of five, identical 16th century **Iznik tiles,** with prominent *saz* leaf design. These were trophies, acquired by sailors and merchants, and included as decoration.

By taking the alley-way out of the south corner of the terrace beside the church, and then descending to the left, you are confronted after 100m by one of the most remarkable churches in Chora—***Aghios Michaïl**, whose exterior is a veritable museum of ancient fragments, sarcophagi, column sections and inscriptions.

Immediately visible are the large **slabs of sarcophagus** (c. 190 x 70 cm: 5 in total on the east and west façades, plus two lids immured to either side of the window over the west door), carved with bold designs of abstract ornamental forms based on garland and altar motifs. The pale purple volcanic stone from which they are carved (somewhat like a poor man's porphyry) reveals their origin from Assos in Turkey, a little to the south of Troy. They are probably work of the 2nd or 1st century BC. The east end of the church incorporates other elements: part of a boss from a marble coffer, a run of egg and dart cornice, and an ancient marble slab with two rosettes, carved with a partially legible inscription of the 2nd century BC referring to a certain 'Praxiteles, son of Praxiteles'. The corners of the church and the west front incorporate more ancient, largely white marble elements. The interior is unusually light; it contains fine icons and icon-frames, and two large carved marble candlesticks.

At this point you are once again close the water front, dominated by the **Demarcheion** (Town Hall): it has a broad, low roof of schist 'slates' and a delicate first-floor balcony, giving pleasing relief to the façade.

OUTER CHORA

The remaining churches of interest in Chora are far-
ther flung. Inland of the southern end of the waterfront
(beyond *Plateia Platanos*), is the 18th century church of
the **Panaghia Eleftherótria**, which, like Aghios Michaïl,
also incorporates sarcophagus slabs from the same Assos
workshop, together with Early Christian fragments and a
variety of 19th century ceramic plates embedded in the
exterior walls. On the south wall is a cypress-tree design
in brick-tiles. The large church of the Dormition of the
Virgin, known as the **Panaghia 'Papameletíou'**, recognisable by its high tiled octagonal drum with double rows
of arches above the window-lights in the cupola, lies
in the upper central area of the Chora. The church was
built in the 1670s, and has been restored in recent years;
inside there is remarkable wood carving in the iconostasis and the throne. Between this church and the other
large church of the Tris Gerarches to its north, and in the
streets below and to the south of the *kastro*, are many substantial and prosperous **houses** with a variety of characteristic wooden balconies. Some still conserve roofs in the
traditional stone from Pelion. They bear witness to the
discreet wealth of Skopelos in the 19th century.

The **Skopelos Folklore Museum** (*open daily 10–1*)

lies in the centre of town, northwest of Platanos Square and of the church of Aghios Merkourios. Given the prosperity and diversity of traditions of the island, its offerings are somewhat limited. It is laid out in a traditional Skopelos house which has unpainted wooden balconies on the exterior, and a plain interior. The first two floors are dedicated to exhibiting a variety of tools, looms, costumes, textiles, photographs and ceramics, illustrative of the island's customs. The textiles are the most striking, especially the women's colourful betrothal dresses. The top floor has an interesting didactic display of the feasts of the year, month by month, on Skopelos.

Other than the walls at the *kastro* and a number of dispersed fragments incorporated into later churches, the visible remains of Classical *Peparethos* are scant. Five hundred metres along the shore to the south of the centre of Chora, before the *Sea View Hotel*, are the remains of an **Asklepieion**, built some way outside of the ancient town as was usual with sanctuaries frequented by the infirm. It profited from curative and thermal springs by the shore. Excavations here (which have since been covered over again) brought to light the foundations of a *stoa* and many votive offerings and figurines. The traces of buildings once visible on the beach are now gone, and only a fragment of a prostrate column and the base of a temple, oriented on the cardinal points, remain to be seen from what was an important 4th century sanctuary and healing centre.

THE SOUTH AND EAST OF THE ISLAND

THE EASTERN MONASTERIES

The shoreline road which passes the Asklepieion is the only access to the eastern extremity of the island and the group of monasteries on the slopes of Mount Palouki (567m). Apart from the historic and architectural interest of this group of five monasteries, the journey to them is panoramic and the final walk to the monastery of the Taxiarches is through wild and untouched coastal scenery.

The **monastery of the Evangelismós** (the Annunciation) (3.5km. *Open daily 8–1 & 4–8*) is a 17th century building on the site of an older foundation, in a position commanding impressive views over the bay of the Chora: it now has three resident nuns. From outside, the attractive cupola drum of the *catholicon* is visible, studded with Ottoman ceramic plates (from Iznik and Çanakkale). It is ironic that a Christian monastic foundation constructed in a period of Moslem Turkish occupation should conspicuously display these unmistakable pieces of 'Ottomania': they were primarily decorative, but they also served as a tacit sign of compliance to avert any malign intentions of the overlords. The door to the *catholicon* has elaborate late 17th century carved lintels, but plain columns and capitals supporting the dome inside. The most unusual element of the interior is the **polychrome tile floor**, which dates from not long after the original construction. The tiles, set in rather erratic design, are a kind that was popular in Sicily and Southern Italy in the 18th century. The kitchen on the north side of the monastery buildings has a fine example of a large bread oven.

Across the valley is the **monastery of the Metamórphosis** (the Transfiguration) (4km. *Open daily 8.30–1.30 & 5.30–8*). Like the Evangelismós this is a dependency of the Xeropotamos Monastery on Mount Athos, but is an older foundation going back to c. 1500. It has a more compact feel, and the simple steeply domed interior of the *catholicon* is adorned by a beautiful carved 17th century iconostasis. One monk remains in the monastery.

Both the road and the footpath beyond the Metamorphosis reach a plateau where a landscape populated with chapels and monastic settlements opens out: the mid-

17th century, fortress-like **Aghia Barbara**, and beyond it, the nunnery of **Aghios Ioannis Prodromos** (St John the Baptist) (6km. *Open daily: 8–1 & 5–8*). A restoration project is underway at Aghia Barbara and the whole construction is now visible in its bare unplastered stone, giving it more the look of a fortress than ever. The cruciform *catholicon* has three curious apses which are linked over their conical roofs by a 'flying' gutter, which collects and channels rainwater from the roof into a cistern. Aghios Ioannis Prodromos was founded slightly earlier in 1612, but then enlarged and restored in 1721, the date it bears over the door. Founded as a male monastery, it became a nunnery in 1920, and now has three resident nuns. The *catholicon* here has a painted iconostasis with beautifully carved symbolic animals of the Byzantine bestiary. The icon of St John the Baptist is also worthy of note.

Beyond these two monasteries, a track, with fine views of Alonnisos, continues for a further 2km: it passes a junction which leads down to the modern chapel of Aghia Triada, and comes to a point (7km) where a path leads steeply downhill to the east (left) towards the church of Aghia Anna, and then branches right for the *monastery of the Taxiarches** (c. 8km). This tiny monastery or hermitage is sewn in a crease of the mountain, about 30 minutes south from the beginning of the path, which leads through a dense maquis of arbutus trees. Like many other places dedicated to the Archangels, it is built beside the entrance of a cave-like breach in the hillside, from which two springs flow out with a good sweet water. There are small monastery buildings around the *catholicon* which has the simple dome on a cube form, with an apse which has been restored—possibly added—at a later date. The main curiosity here lies in the carved, large-bellied **figure-heads** which protrude from the ogival bell-tower. There is complete isolation and peace here: the only sound is from the running water of the springs.

SOUTH OF CHORA TO STAFILOS

(Chora = 0.0km for distances in text)

Almost due south of the waterfront, a good asphalt road leads into the fertile valley of Stáfilos, an area which has always been used for the cultivation of the fresh produce and cereals needed by the main town. At **Stáfilos Bay** (4km), on the island's south coast, a beach stretches to the east where a conspicuous headland projects south into the sea, attached by a narrow isthmus to the shore. It is beside this steep promontory, with its classic 'acropolis' form, that a **Middle Bronze Age shaft-grave** (c. 1500 BC),

complete with burial gifts and objects, was uncovered in
1936. The grave itself (now mostly refilled), which was located just to the west of the isthmus of the headland, was
damaged but contained a magnificent Mycenaean gold
handle of a sword, now exhibited in the National Archaeological Museum in Athens. This and other objects which
were found suggested an important, royal burial, which
was subsequently dubbed that of 'King Staphylos', the leg-
endary ruler of the island, and son of Ariadne by either
Theseus or Dionysos. Access and exploration of the headland is more difficult than it seems because of the dense
vegetation: near the triangulation point on the summit
there are areas of collapsed ancient stone. Beyond the
headland, further to the east is the long **beach of Velanió**.

From Stáfilos, the main road climbs to the west into
dense pine woods that cover the whole of the west and
the centre of the island, to the protected port of **Ag-
nontas** (7.5km) named after Hagnon, a victorious ath-
lete from *Peparethos* in the Olympic Games of 569 BC. A
coastal road from here leads (1km) to the beautiful **beach
of Limnonari**. The main road climbs inland again and
reaches a junction (10km), where the right turn heads
back towards Chora. As it descends into the valley, the
monastery of Aghios Reginos is on the left. The cult of St
Reginus, who was one of the first evangelists of Christian-

ity on the island, goes back to the time of his martyrdom at the end of the reign of Julian the Apostate (in 362/363 AD). A first church on this site may have been built shortly after that date to enshrine the sarcophagus in which he was buried. The existing church here is a renovated structure of the 18th century, but the presence of many early Christian columns in the forecourt indicates that it is built on the site of a much earlier construction. Into one of the columns beside the steps in the forecourt is cut a curious version of the **sacred acronym** 'ΙΧΘΥΣ', in which the five letters are compressed and joined into a single hieroglyph, with more the appearance of a fossilised insect than the usual symbolic fish.

On reaching the outskirts of Chora again, the massive, buttressed façade of a ruined monastery building looms above the road on the left: the carved stone supports of what was once a wide balcony can be seen projecting from the centre of the façade at the top. This is the **Episkopí Monastery** (*normally closed, except by arrangement with the owners*). As residence of the bishop, this was the most important monastery on the island. It is now a private residence. The present 17th century single-aisled church of the Panaghia inside the walls is built on the site of the northern aisle of a much larger three-aisled Early Christian basilica of the 5th or 6th century, which was renovated or reconstructed—according to an inscription in the wall of the present church—in 1078, when a certain Anastasios was Bishop of Skopelos. It seems probable that the original basilica was constructed on the site of a pre-existing ancient sanctuary and used marble elements from it.

From the Episkopí Monastery, it is less than half a kilometre back to the peripheral road around Chora. Taking this road to the north (left), which climbs steeply around the back of the town to the Kastro, brings you to the point where the next itinerary begins.

THE NORTH OF THE ISLAND

MOUNT DELPHI AND SENDOUKIA

From the northern extremity of the peripheral road around the Chora of Skopelos, a narrow road leads north and west into the island's interior towards its highest peak, Mount Delphi (681m), and its densest woods, the Váthia Forest. (*Follow indications for 'Sendoukia' and for the monasteries in this area.*) After 1km the road runs along the side of a fertile valley with olive trees: on the opposite side, screened by ancient cypress trees, is the small **monastery of the Koimisis tis Theotokou** (the Dormition of the Virgin). At the western head of this valley (3km), a track leads off the asphalt road to the west, and climbs rapidly through dense pinewoods, past the **springs** at Karyá: taking this track, 600m after the springs, a right hand fork leads down to the extensive complex of the **monastery of Aghios Efstathios** (7km), a well-preserved foundation of 1596, with a simple and unpainted church of an inscribed-cross plan, with more recently added monastery buildings to its north which are used as a retreat by a community in Thessaloniki. There is a palpable peacefulness in these valleys, broken only by the sounds of goatherds calling. **Mount Delphi** dominates to the northwest, its massive slopes softened by the thick covering of Aleppo pines and arbutus, broken in the valleys by stands of plane and cypress trees.

Returning to the junction for Aghios Efstathios, the road climbs on up towards the summit and, at a fork in the tracks (6.5km), the path to *Sendoukia (meaning 'boxes' or 'chests') is clearly signed to the right and thereafter marked by a series of small stone cairns. It leads eventually to the northern tip of a long limestone outcrop on the shoulder of the mountain, which ends with a sudden drop to the east and magnificent *views of Alonnisos. Just by the edge of the drop are four empty graves: three deep and precisely carved *loculi* (approximately 1.80 x 0.90m, and 0.85m deep), with solid stone roofs of a highly pitched profile, and one shallow excavated rectangular area—probably an uncompleted grave (or possibly the base for a stone monument or sarcophagus which was either never completed or has since disappeared). All are oriented due east. In each of the *loculi* is a shallow 'ledge' at the western end: the rim is also carefully drafted all the way around for the snug fitting of the lid.

A bewildering spread of dates has been ascribed to these graves by scholars, some putting them as early as the Neolithic period, others as late as the early Christian era. The best evidence is the physical appearance of the cutting of the rock. The fine precision of the right-angle corners, the cleanness of the edges, the vestiges of bevelling and drafting, and the density of fine chisel striations on the insides of the *loculi* would point to a date neither earlier than advanced Classical workmanship (c. 400 BC) nor later than mid-Imperial Roman workmanship (c. 200 AD). The scale, the obvious pleasure taken in precision and proportion, and the kind of tools which appear to have been used all suggest work of the Hellenistic period. The design of the lids, with their highly pitched profiles, also seems to be influenced by designs from southwest Asia Minor of the 4th and 3rd centuries BC. The graves may be part of a larger monumental or cultic area: on the eminence above them (100m due west of the graves) is a conical shaped mound in the natural limestone which shows signs of cutting in the bedrock, possibly for an altar or shrine related to the graves below.

It is difficult to say for certain why this particular site—and not, for example, the summit of Mount Delphi, or an eminence above the city, or above the coast—was chosen. It is remote and apparently unrelated to any wider human presence There may be significance in the open view to Alonnisos or in the orientation due east into the equinoctial sunrise. We understand little about the reasons for the positioning of sanctuaries and temples in Antiquity, and even less about the choice of burial sites such as this.

From the junction near to Sendoukia, the mountain tracks lead in several directions through the forests on the slopes of Mount Delphi. The track to the northwest skirts the whole mountain (15.5km). From the junction, signposted to Pyrgos, at the southern point of the loop, a winding track leads 6 km down to the west coast at Pánormos. Alternatively the same point can be reached by returning to Skopelos Chora and taking the main asphalt road south west to Pánormos.

PANORMOS, GLOSSA AND AROUND CAPE GOUROUNI

The west coast of the island is characterised by bay after bay of azure water, thick pinewoods descending to the shore and a general sparseness of building. The hidden natural bay and the protected coastal valley at **Pánormos** (11.5km) was an ideal site for a city in Antiquity. Ancient *Pánormos* was founded by colonists from Chalcis in the 7th century BC at roughly the same time as *Peparethos*, as part of a determined policy by the mother city to reinforce and protect her vital trading routes towards the northern Aegean Sea. The settlement was clustered around an acropolis on the rise in the centre of the sweep of the valley, about half way along the shore line. Stretches of **Classical walling** can be seen on the north slope of the hill, though hidden by the growth of olive and pine trees. These are best viewed from the road, as you descend to Pánormos beach from the north, and are located just above and behind the Pánormos Beach Hotel. (*To reach the acropolis on foot, take the concrete driveway which leads inland from the centre of the main front at Pánormos towards the Hotel Afroditi. At the point where the road ends, a path continues: by cutting back from the path to the left over the hill, you reach the walls.*) The site, with the remains of two round towers and a gate amongst the vegetation and pines, stretches back along the ridge. The city extended to the south in the valley below: at the valley's eastern extremity is a cave which in Antiquity may have been a **sanctuary to Pan**. Along the shore to the south of the bay, the shallow and hidden inlet of **Blo** (probably a corruption of the ancient Greek root πλέω, 'sail'), was the site of the city's protected harbour.

North of Pánormos are a number of **beaches** with limpid water of aquamarine colour: **Miliá, Kastáni, Fteliá**. The road passes Élios (18km), or 'Nea (new) Klima', a planned settlement created and developed in the 1970s after the earthquake of 1965 devastated the village of (Old) Klima, to the north. **Klima** itself (22km), is a small settlement of traditional stone houses with wooden balconies—now extensively restored—with panoramic views towards Skiathos, Euboea and the Pelion massif. **Glóssa** (24.5km) also has a similar vernacular architecture to that found on the mainland around Mount Pelion. It sits in a panoramic dip in the hill, just above the rise which was occupied by the acropolis of Ancient *Selinoús*—the third and last Chalcidian colony of the 7th century BC on Skopelos. Remains of the ancient city's walls can be seen directly in front on the hillside, just before reaching the last hairpin bend on the descent into **Loutráki** (27.5km).

The remains of **Ancient *Selinoús*** at Loutráki are sparse and spread out. What is visible to the visitor mostly dates from the Roman period, when *Selinoús* was a flourishing commercial port. At the far southeastern end of the shore are the remains of the 3rd century AD **Roman baths**. By walking along the rocks after the path ends, it is possible to see sections of the back wall in *opus mixtum*, a part of the hypocaust furnace, and small areas of pebble floor-mosaic. This was a recreational centre for both mineral water bathing and sea bathing, which would have incorporated a *gymnasium* and areas for social and cultural gatherings. Much of the construction has been washed away together with the shore that has suffered from earthquake degradation; the rest remains unexcavated under the cliff. Other Roman vestiges are to be found in the area: the remains of an arched *stoa* from the town's *agorá* inland of the port, the upper part of which carried an aqueduct. Evidence of a later, Early Christian presence is evident at the church of Aghios Nikolaos beside the harbour, where fragments of early Byzantine architectural members, decorated with palm and acanthus motifs, can be seen in the forecourt of the church.

Turning back up the steep hill on the asphalt road by which you arrived, you come at the eastern extremity of Glóssa to a point where there are two junctions with roads

to the north. The first leads to the northern extremity of
the island. After 2km, it passes the **monastery of the Taxi-
archis** (26.5km), a now deserted monastery in a superb
position, with a small 17th century *catholicon*. The early
Byzantine columns here come from a 7th century church
on this site. Seven kilometres beyond the road ends at the
square tower of the **Gourouni lighthouse** (34.5km). This
is a piece of interesting industrial architecture, built in
1889. The careful design of its decagonal lantern, castel-
lated observation balcony and rusticated edges and windows, goes pleasingly beyond the requirements of mere
functionality.

Archaeological mapping of this northernmost promontory of the island has revealed that the 19th century
lighthouse is only the latest in a long tradition of lookout
posts in the area: there appears to have been a network of
fortified agricultural buildings and towers here from as
early as the 4th century BC. Separated by less than a kilometre and clearly visible from one another, these struc-
tures were important in safeguarding both agricultural
activity in the area and protecting the important trade-
routes through the sea at this point.

From the eastern extremity of Glóssa, the second junction leads 5.5km to the east coast through steep and forested valleys down to the shore at the isolated and evoca-

tive church of **Aghios Ioannis sto Kastrí,** built on top of a rock protruding into the sea, and accessible only by a flight of steps. The interest and beauty of the place lie less in the church and its few monastic cells than in the journey to it and its dramatic setting on one of the island's wildest stretches of coast.

PRACTICAL INFORMATION

370 03 **Skopelos:** area 95sq. km; perimeter 102km; resident population 4706; max. altitude 681 m. **Port Authorities:** T. 24240 22180 (Chora) & T. 33033 (Glóssa). **Tourist information:** Thalpos Holidays, T. 24240 29036, fax 23057, www.skopelos.gr

ACCESS

By boat: Skopelos has no airport; access is by ferry (4–5 hrs) and hydrofoil (approx. 2 hrs) from the port of Volos, from which there are several daily services both to Glóssa at the northwestern tip of the island and to the main port of Skopelos, There are also less frequent connections to the mainland, closer to Athens, from Aghios Konstantinos (5 times a week; same journey times as from Volos), and from Kymi on Euboea (2 times a week). Skopelos is only 70 minutes by ferry or 45 minutes by hydrofoil from Skiathos, which is served by daily flights from Athens: if a good connection is made, this can be the fastest way to Skopelos from the capital. The island lies on the route between Skiathos and Alonnisos, and nearly all of the services which call at Skopelos also communicate with these islands.

LODGING

Approximately 500m east of the port of Skopelos along the shore, is the **Hotel Prince Stafilos**, set back in the peace of its own gardens, this is the most luxurious and tasteful of the island's hotels in the higher price range (*T. 24240 22775 & 22744, fax 22825, www.prince-stafilos.gr*); alternatively, very central and economical lodgings can be found on the front opposite the port, at the **Hotel Adonis**, but there is the possibility of restaurant noise at night (*T. 24240 22231, fax 23239*). Simple accommodations, a fine view over the town, and very welcoming family hospitality are offered at the **Thea Home Studios**, at the top of the peripheral road, west of the port

(*T. 24240 22859, fax 23556*). Alternatively, for peace and a beautiful setting right on the beach, **Limnonari Studios** are ideal and welcoming (*T. 24240 23854, fax 22242, e-mail limnonari@skopelos.net*). Also not far from the shore on the west coast of the island, there is the **Pánormos Beach Hotel** at Pánormos, 12km from Skopelos Chora (*T. 24240 22711, fax 23366, www. Pánormosbeach-hotel.gr*).

EATING

The most thoughtful and creative taverna on Skopleos is **Agnanti* at Glóssa, mixing traditional Greek dishes with new ideas, in a setting with delightful views. Simpler homemade dishes, fresh wine and island-fare can be found at the taverna **Terpsis,** just outside Stafilos on the road to Chora. The taverna is family-run and has a shady garden for eating outside; it specializes mostly in vegetable *mezédes* and meat dishes.

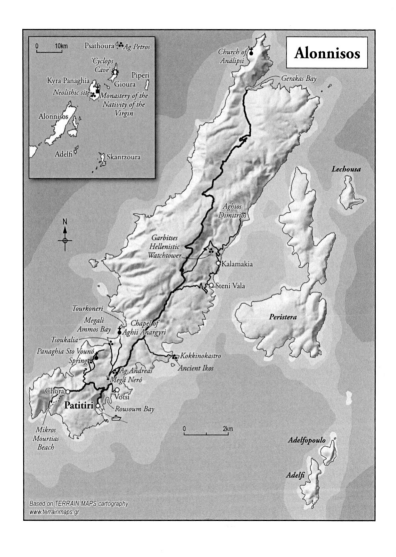

Alonnisos

0   10km

Psathoura •••Ag Petros

'Cyclops
Cave'   Piperi
Kyra Panaghia ↑   Gioura
Neolithic site   Monastery of the
                  Nativity of the
                      Virgin
Alonnisos

Adelfi   Skantzoura

Church of
Análipsi

Gerakas Bay

Lechousa

Aghios
Dimitriós

N

Garbitses
Hellenistic
Watchtower
                      ⚓ Kalamakia

                    ⚓ Steni Vala

Peristera

Tourkoneri
Megali
Ammos Bay   Chapel of
Tsoukalia   Aghii Anargyri
Panaghia Sto Vounó
Springs
              ⚓ Kokkinokastro
          Ag. Andreas   Ancient Ikos
          Mega Neró
Chora ○   ○ Votsi
     Patitiri   Rousoum Bay

Mikros   Adelfopoulo
Mourtias
Beach

0   2km
                        Adelfi

Based on TERRAIN MAPS cartography
www.terrainmaps.gr

ALONNISOS

Alonnisos has a stronger scent of pine and wild oregano in its air than almost any other island. Its waters are limpid, its forests intact, and its coastline—indented with enchanting coves and beaches—mostly un-built. Lovers of walking and swimming, and those who appreciate the attractions of simplicity have not failed to notice this. After centuries of obscurity, Alonnisos has acquired a new sense of identity through the creation of the largest Marine Conservation Area in Europe: it encompasses the whole island and the scattering of islets to its north and east. This aims to protect the area's rare wildlife and the notable fecundity of its waters from the ecological upset caused by development and mass recreation. Far from discouraging tourism, the 'Northern Sporades Marine Park' aims to create a new kind of alternative tourism based on respect for the environment and interest in its unique natural riches. Walkers, snorkelers and sailors frequent Alonnisos in large numbers in the summer. Other visitors come in connection with the *International Academy of Classical Homeopathy* established on the island in 1994, which represents yet another aspect of the characteristically nature-oriented philosophy of the island.

The constantly varying profiles and vegetation of the smaller islands around Alonnisos constitute a marine landscape of exceptional beauty. There is an intimacy to their waters which has appealed to human settlers and traders from the very beginnings of human history. Neolithic (and earlier) archaeology in the area is of great importance, and some of the Aegean's richest prehistoric sites are scattered among the outlying islands. Such a landscape offered early man a fruitful equilibrium between the natural protection afforded by an island in the sea and the ease of communication and commerce which the sea facilitated. It is the story of Greek civilisation in microcosm. Though quiet today, these waters were a busy and important commercial thoroughfare throughout Antiquity: the number and the size of the ancient shipwrecks found on the sea-bed here are ample confirmation.

Outside the busy port and the rapidly reviving Chora, the island has tranquil shores and a landscape of charm and natural beauty. Alonnisos and its diaspora of islets represent the eastern boundary of the land-mass of central mainland Greece. At this extremity, the broken land merges with the open sea. Beyond—and on occasions just visible—lies the different world of the eastern islands along the coast of Asia.

HISTORY

Some of the earliest evidence found so far of human presence in the Aegean area, dating from c. 10,000 BC, has been unearthed in the 'Cave of the Cyclops' on the island of Gioura to the northeast of Alonnisos: and the earliest organised Neolithic settlements have been explored around the Bay of Aghios Petros on Kyra Panaghia, and at Kokkinokastro on Alonnisos. The island was later settled by pre-Greek peoples, Carians and Dolopians. In historic times Alonnisos—called *Ikos* throughout Classical Antiquity—was, like Skiathos and Skopelos, a 7th century BC colony of Chalcis on Euboea. The 6th century BC writer and explorer, Scylax of Caryanda, mentions there being two cities on the island. The range in productivity of the Sporades islands can be seen in the fact that *Ikos*, as a member of the First Athenian League from 478 BC, was assessed at 1,500 drachmae in annual tithe, as opposed to 1,000 drachmae for *Skiathos*, and 18,000 drachmae (3 talents) for *Peparethos* (Skopelos). Having been allies of Athens in the Peloponnesian War, the Northern Sporades were subsequently occupied by Sparta. *Ikos* regained independence and was a member of the 2nd Athenian League until its dissolution in 346 BC. In 355 BC the neighbouring island of *Halonnesos* (probably to be identified as ancient Kyra Panaghia) was occupied by the pirate Sostrates; he was later expelled by the Macedonians, who built a fort on the island in 343 BC. *Halonnesos* became a bone of contention between Philip II of Macedon and the Athenians, and the issue is the subject of one of the orations of Demosthenes (*Or.* VII). In the settlement following the Battle of Chaeronea in 338 BC the Sporades along with Northern Greece fell under Macedonian supremacy. The island of *Ikos*, along with Skiathos and Skopelos, was devastated by Philip V of Macedon in 220 BC in his attempt to render them of no strategic use to his adversaries the Romans, who nonetheless became masters of the region after 146 BC. Mark Anthony later ceded the islands to Athens in gratitude for the city's military support.

Christianity must have come to the island around the time of the martyrdom of St Reginus on Skopelos in 362/3 AD, but the island was even more exposed than most to the destructive Slav and Arab incursions into the Aegean during the 7th and 8th centuries. In 1204, after the 4th Crusade, the island now apparently called '*Chelidromia*', came under the possession of the Venetian Ghisi family together with the other Sporades islands. In 1276 they were driven out by the Veronese admiral Licario, acting on behalf of

Constantinople, and the island was returned to Byzantine control up until 1453. After the fall of Constantinople the inhabitants sought the protection of the Venetian Republic, which subsequently governed the island, except for a decade of Turkish occupation between 1475 and 1486, until 1538 when it was ransacked and finally captured for the Turks by Khaireddin Barbarossa. During the following centuries the outer islands of the Sporades suffered particularly from piracy; but they enjoyed tax privileges bestowed by Osman III in 1756. In 1821, in the course of the Greek War of Independence, a free 'Demos Alonnisou' under the jurisdiction of the new Greek administration of the Sporades was declared. The island was officially ceded to the Greek State by Turkey in 1830.

In 1965 the island's main centre of population at Chora was badly damaged by a severe earthquake; the population was moved to Patitíri, in the area of the harbour. In May 1992, the 'National Marine Park of Alonissos - Northern Sporades' (NMPANS) was established by Presidential decree to protect the landscape and waters of the area, and the habitats of rare and threatened species of plant and animal—most especially the Mediterranean monk seal (Monachus monachus). In 1994 George Vithoulkas established the centre of the International Academy of Classical Homeopathy on Alonnisos.

PATITIRI

The name of the island's main harbour reveals something of the history of the island. A '*patitírion*' is a place where grapes are trodden. Like its larger neighbour, Skopelos, on which it has depended throughout its history, Alonnisos produced and exported wine in Antiquity. Amphorae for the transporting of wine, stamped with the legend 'IKION', implying 'produce of *Ikos*' (the ancient name of Alonnisos), have been found at various points around the Aegean and Black Sea area, and at Alexandria in Egypt. In recent times the successors to those vines were wiped out by philoxera in 1968 and only a small number have since been replanted on the island as new stock. Today **Patitíri** is an unpretentious port, hastily built in the late 1960s and 70s with no particular architectural merit but with a pleasing setting around the attractive harbour-front and the steep slopes that encircle it. It has greater intimacy than the other ports of the Sporades.

Displays of the processes and the apparatus of the island's long tradition of wine-production can be seen in the **Kostas and Angelas Mavriki Museum** (*open daily June–Oct 11–7*), visible above the western side of the harbour in a stone building whose imposing size promises perhaps more than the museum currently delivers.

The collection, neatly displayed over three floors with a café-terrace above, is nonetheless instructive: the '**Pirate Museum**' on the *upper floor* underlines the extent to which the history of the peripheral islands of the Aegean, such as Alonnisos, has been bound up with the perennial scourge of piracy. Manacles, guns, nautical equipment (which includes a fore-runner of barbed-wire for preventing the boarding of pirates on ships) are displayed. On the *ground floor* is the modern historical section, exhibiting arms, shells, mines and other related bellic material and documents. The greatest variety of material is in the *basement*, where artefacts of the island's traditional economy are displayed: **wine-presses** and a **fermentation vat** of remarkable proportions, as well as alembics for preparing distillates. Of particular interest is the **equipment used by pack-saddle makers**, from a time when the accoutrements for mules were as important as those for cars today. The displayed seal-skin sandals once used by islanders are—in view of the island's current dedication to the preservation of the Mediterranean monk seal—a poignant reminder of past habits.

CHORA AND ENVIRONS

A severe earthquake in March 1965, of magnitude 6.3, damaged over 80 per cent of the buildings on Alonnisos: it caused seismic waves in the sea which were observed on Kyra Panaghia at the time. As a result of this *Chora, the picturesque hill-top capital of the island, was abandoned and its small harbour hastily adapted and built up into today's settlement of Patitíri. Much of the old settlement, whose position is one of the finest in the Sporades, has been sensitively restored and revitalised, even if a slightly artificial air prevails owing to the fact that it is principally a summer retreat for visitors. The short distance to Chora from the port (3km by road) can be covered by foot (1.5km, 30 minutes) along the old mule-path. The main part of the settlement is preceded by a charming *plateia*, with cypress and mulberry trees, balconied houses, a war memorial, and a handsome neoclassical façade hidden slightly behind the long, low 17th century **church of Aghios Athanasios**. The windows of the church have curiously pointed frames, and the row of blind pointed arches along the north wall would suggest that some structure, perhaps a *parecclesion*, has been removed. Across the square to the left side is the settlement's principal place of worship, the Christoú church, also of the late 17th century and dedicated to the Nativity of Christ: it is a simple domed chamber with a small narthex but no protruding apse, roofed in schist slabs from Pelion. Inside, the wooden balcony reserved for women is still in situ. From here the path climbs steps and the view opens out over the whole of the island to the north: at this higher level, you enter the area of the old 'kastro', roughly bisected by a gracefully curving street, now lined with shops and tavernas, which finishes abruptly at the far end with a different and equally dramatic view, this time towards Skopelos and the south and west. Another narrow crescent street runs parallel to the north side, where the older houses, many abandoned, are built on the edge of the natural fortification of the site. In their midst is the oldest of Chora's churches to have survived, **Aghios Giorgios**, dating probably from the 15th century. It suffered little damage in the earthquake of 1965 beyond the detachment of some plaster which revealed areas of wall-painting beneath. The remaining churches and many of the houses in the web of tiny streets downhill to the south had to be rebuilt after 1965. From Chora a path leads south, steeply down through olives, pines and scrub to the bay of Mikrós Mourtiás, with a sheltered, sandy beach.

About 600m east of Chora, along the road back to Patitíri, is the modern **church of Aghios Ioannis**, standing on a small eminence: the remains of **ancient walls**, some terracing and a path cut in the rock can be seen behind and below the east end of the church and extending a short way down the hill to the north. These are the exiguous remains of the island's second ancient settlement (after *Ikos* on the east coast), whose existence is mentioned in the *Periplous* of Scylax of Caryanda, the late 6th century BC explorer.

Further east, from a point midway between Patitíri and Chora, after the church of Prophitis Elias, a by-road to the left (north) followed by two successive right forks, leads to the rural church of the **Panaghia sto Vounó**, visible in a saddle after a wayside **spring** of soft water (the 'Vrysi tis Panaghias'). The church was founded as a monastery in the late 15th or early 16th century, but abandoned less than two centuries later. Both the setting amidst olive and cypress trees and the simple proportions of the schist-tiled cupola on its square base are particularly beautiful. The interior is plain, apart from fine but damaged **paintings** in the ceiling: the *Pantocrator with Seraphim, Archangels, the Virgin and Baptist*, with *Evangelists and Prophets* below, survive in and around the dome and the drum.

AROUND THE ISLAND

FROM PATITIRI TO THE WEST COAST

Patitíri is the westernmost of a series of three intimate coves in the protected southeast corner of the island: its area of habitation now spreads east behind **Rousoum Bay** (the next cove east), and incorporates the separate neighbourhood of Vótsi (2km) beyond, named after Admiral Nikolaos Votsis (1877–1931), who used Alonnisos as a naval base during the Balkan Wars. A kilometre to the north of Votsi and to the left of the main road is the *International Academy of Classical Homeopathy*, founded and supervised by a widely published and respected homeopathic practitioner and theorist, George Vithoulkas (b. 1932). A little way to its west, ruined architectural fragments mark the site of **Aghios Andreas**, one of the two Early Christian churches which have been located so far on Alonnisos.

In the valley north of Votsi is the island's most abundant **spring**, Megá Neró (*turning to north off main road, 2.1km from Patitíri waterfront*). Beyond the springs a track leads 1.5km across the width of the island to the small bay of **Tsoukaliá** on the generally less protected north coast. A windmill (private) has been reconstructed in the bay.

On the east slope of Tsoukaliá Bay are the vestigial remains of an ancient installation, partially buried in the pine-woods. There is a thick scatter of ancient potsherds (although in places mixed with modern) at the base of the hill. This was the site of a substantial **wine-making installation of the Classical and Hellenistic periods**, with associated pottery workshops producing the amphorae for transportation. (The name '*tsoukaliá*' means 'pots' in modern Greek.) It is here that a number of amphora handles, stamped with the legend 'IKION' have been found, confirming the ancient name of the island as *Ikos*. The rock-cut pool in the bed of the torrent behind the bay was also probably worked and enlarged in Antiquity.

The right-hand branch off the main track, 1km before the Bay of Tsoukaliá, leads north and slightly east for a further 1.5km, at which point a narrow path continues a further 400m to the **hermitage chapel of the Aghii Anargyri**—possibly founded as early as the 15th century—now solitary, without its surrounding cells, on a wooded cliff overlooking the sea. The minute square interior is surmounted by a low cupola, tiled in schist; in the masonry of the corners are immured terracotta pots, ostensibly to emphasise the acoustics. In the hills to south and to east are more springs; below are the beautiful coves of **Tourkonéri** and **Megáli Ámmos**, which are accessible by foot. On the summit of the steep hill, due east of the latter are the remains of the **Hellenistic watchtower** of Kastráki.

THE EAST COAST

The site of **Ancient *Ikos*** is on the point at **Kokkinókastro** (6km), a long peninsula projecting into the sea in the middle of the lower eastern half of the island, defining two sweeping beaches to either side. At sunset, as the headland takes on a deep orange colour, it merits its name of '*kokkino kastro*', or 'red acropolis'. The point of the promontory where the remains of the city are, with its steep seaward cliffs, is attached by a high, razor-thin isthmus of eroding sandstone which effectively denies any access by foot. There are only two means of access—by boat, or by swimming out from the south beach (c. 20 minutes) and climbing ashore at the southeastern point where the headland slopes down to the sea.

The tip of the headland is indented by a deep cove, which served as a protected roadstead. Cutting transversely across the lower slopes is a fine **stretch of fortification wall** in high Classical 5th century BC masonry, which has recently been

cleared and excavated. There is a dense scatter of potsherds
and evidence of foundations and walls, still buried, further
up the slope to the west. Archaeological exploration has also
revealed a far earlier Palaeolithic and Mesolithic human
presence on the peninsula, as well as on the offshore island
of **Kokkinónisi** to the south, where evidence of Neolithic
and Bronze Age settlements has also been found.

Continuing north on the principal road through the
wooded interior of the island, a right turn from a junction 7.5km from Patitíri leads down to the east coast at
Steni Vala (11km), a tranquil creek with a harbour, front-
ed by excellent tavernas. The principal *Monk Seal Rescue
Centre* is based here. One kilometre further north on the
main island road beyond the Steni Vala junction, a track
(right) leads 2.2 km down a valley to the site of Garbitses
where the circular base, standing to a height of only three
courses, of a **Late Classical watchtower** lies in low scrub,
200m to the east of the track. The track continues a further 1km, before rejoining the asphalt continuation of
the Steni Vala road along the coast. Two and a half kilometres further north along the coast on this road is the
flat reedy promontory of **Aghios Dimitrios**, where there
are the (scarcely visible) remains of a three aisled **Early
Christian basilica** which stood here. The basilica was the

centre of a small community, with houses and baths. As often with Christian churches built in the Islands before the Arab invasions of the 7th and 8th centuries, it stood in an unprotected position beside the shore. There are particularly attractive **beaches** at Aghios Dimitrios. Four kilometres to the north—visitable only by small boat—are a number of shore-level **caves and grottos**, once common refuges for the monk-seals.

The northern half of the island is a landscape of steep, wooded gorges alternating with areas of low maquis with Phoenician juniper and tree heather: it is mostly uninhabited apart from scattered farmsteads. The main axial road that runs the length of the island terminates in the deep creek of **Gerákas Bay** (20km), where one of the Biological Research Stations of the Marine Park (*see below*) is located. On a cliff at the northwestern extremity of the island is the dilapidated monastery church of the **Analipsi**, founded in the 17th century. The path to it is ruinous, and the church can now only be reached from the sea when the water is calm.

THE LESSER SPORADES (OUTER ISLANDS)

To the north and east of Alonnisos is a scattering of diverse and characterful islands which together form a marine landscape of exceptional beauty. They differ from one another quite markedly—Peristéra is bare and waterless, while Pipéri is densely wooded with pines; Gioúra is mountainous and with dramatic limestone cliffs, while Psathoúra is flat, sandy and with volcanic litter; and Skántzoura is different again with its brilliant marble shores. What they have in common is that they are all largely uninhabited and are kept that way by virtue of their recent incorporation into an enforced conservation area—the **Northern Sporades Marine Park**—which covers a total area of 2,260sq.km. The flagship motivation of the conservation area is the protection of the habitat of the Mediterranean monk seal, Europe's most endangered marine mammal; but there are many corals, cetaceans, birds, goats, cliff and marine plants which also importantly benefit from the protection.

The Marine Park is not solely an area of wildlife conservation, however: it also covers an area of land and water of immense archaeological importance. In a way which bears striking similarities with the history and archaeology of the Lesser Cyclades—a similarly scattered and diverse marine landscape—these tiny unpromising islands were a centre of remarkable human activity in Neolithic times and earlier. Evidence of the earliest human activity in the Aegean is to be found here. The area is also of interest to archaeologists of very different periods because of the large number of shipwrecks in its waters from Ancient, Byzantine and more recent times. In short this fascinating landscape has been a hive of human commerce, exchange and transportation since the beginning of time. It is a microcosm of island culture in general which centres on the sea and its power to connect individual settlements, while endowing them at the same time with a clear sense of individuality.

Modern developments have fortunately passed the islands by, leaving their waters less affected by the ecological ravages that have prevailed elsewhere in the Aegean and the Mediterranean. Now, through the creation of the Northern Sporades Marine Park, they may have acquired the hope of remaining intact for some time to come.

Peristéra lies athwart the eastern coast of Alonnisos. The islet's successive names *Xeró* ('dry', 'barren'), *Sarakinikó* ('of the Saracens or pirates') and *Perisitéra* ('doves') succinctly describe its geography, its history and its unusual shape respectively. The waters of the island were the site of the discovery of the earliest and largest, **5th century BC, shipwrecked vessel** found in the Aegean—located in the late 1980s and first systematically examined in 1991. The Athenian trade-vessel, carrying a cargo of several thousand amphorae of wine from Macedonia, Alonnisos and Skopelos, as well as a considerable quantity of Attic pottery, measured approximately 30 x 10m, with an estimated weight of 150 tons.

Kyrá Panaghiá,12km to the northeast, is thought possibly to have born the name Halonnesos in Antiquity—one of several possible candidates for the name. There is some surface water and the island is consequently covered in dense *maquis*, with breaks of *Quercus coccifera* (the Kerm or Holly oak) in the interior. The large **monastery of the Nativity of the Virgin**, first founded in the 16th century, lies on the island's east coast. During the course of the last century the monastery and its agricultural production dwindled and were finally abandoned, but then taken in hand and restored in the last decade. It is now undergoing a revival and is inhabited almost year round. On the western side of the island is the deep bay of Aghios Petros. Its entrance is partially closed by the island of **Phangroú**, where another important **Classical shipwreck**, with a cargo of wine amphorae, similar in many respects to the Peristera wreck, has been found and explored. In the eastern portion of the bay, the earliest excavated **Neolithic settlement** in the Aegean (5th millennium BC) has been uncovered (1970/71). (See *'Aghios Petros etc.'* Nikos Efstratiou, *B.A.R. International Series*, #241:1985). The site yielded important pottery and distinctive clay figurines. The finds showed the remarkable and unexpected degree of organisation and productivity of the vital culture which evolved in this archipelago in prehistoric times.

Gioúra, further to the northeast, has revealed an even earlier human presence, c. 9000–6000 BC. Excavations in the floor of the '**Cyclops Cave**' (1992–96) in the interior of the south of the island have yielded, from the deepest strata, beautifully fashioned fish-hooks from animal bones (now in the Volos Archaeological Museum), together with bones and skeletons of large fish showing that the technology of fishing was already mastered at this early date. Evidence also suggests that animal husbandry (pigs, goats and sheep) was practised by the early part of this period. There are many caves and unusual limestone phenomena on Gioúra: the mythical association with the Cyclops may have grown up around a curious and large circular perforation which completely pierces a scarp of

rock about 40m above water-level. The forehead-shaped
bulge of rock has the uncanny appearance of a gigantic
brow with a single central eye. Gioúra's impressive rock
faces are home to a variety of unique chasmophytes or
cliff-growing plants, including the very rare, endemic
sandwort *Arenaria phitosiana*. Other rarities include
Campanula reiseri; a scabious, *Scabiosa hymetta*; and a
dwarf fritillary with dark purple flower, *Fritillaria spora-
dum*. About 500 examples of an endemic **species of goat**,
Capra aegagrus, similar to the Cretan *kri-kri* but a little
larger, roam the island.

Psathoúra—which lies 15km due north of Gioúra is as
flat as Gioúra is mountainous. It has shores of white sand
which contrast with its dark native rocks of volcanic an-
desite. Its shallow dunes are a natural home for the beautiful and rare sea daffodil, *Pancratium maritimum*. In the
water off the sandy eastern shore of the island stones dis-
posed in the form of foundations have been interpreted
as the remains of a city which has become submerged
beneath the sea. Based upon this evidence, an interesting and plausible theory has been put forward suggesting
that Psathoúra is in fact the submerged island of *Chryse*
where according to Sophocles, Philoctetes the archer was
bitten by a snake and abandoned by his comrades, and

which Pausanias says was engulfed by the waves (*Descrip.* VIII.33.4) and disappeared under the sea. The hypothesis sits well with other unsolved problems of ancient topography and taxonomy. But it is difficult to square with Pausanias's phrase that *Chryse* was 'no long sail from Lemnos': the islands are separated by almost 100km of open sea. Other theories suggest that Psathoúra was the ancient '*Halonnesos*', whose ownership was a bone of contention between Philip of Macedon and the Athenians: the issue is the subject of one of Demosthenes's surviving orations of 342 BC. Psathoúra marks the northernmost extremity of the Sporades, and the end of an island chain which, via Euboea, facilitates navigation all the way back into the heart of the Cyclades. Its northern tip is marked by a handsome **lighthouse** constructed of local stone in 1895: at just over 26m, it is the highest in the Aegean.

Pipéri, lies well to the east, and is the most intensively protected zone of the whole Marine Park. This steep and well-wooded island represents a particularly important habitat for many of the important protected species: the caves along its shore for the monk seal, and its cliffs for rare chasmophyte plants, sea-birds and raptors. It is thought to be home to over 300 pairs of Eleanora's falcon, which breed in the late summer and feed on small migrating birds through the autumn. Pipéri is also home to Bonelli's eagle, buzzard and Peregrine falcon.

Skántzoura, which lies to the south of the group, together with its outlying rocks and islets, is one of the most important breeding habitats in the Aegean for the rare Audouin's gull (distinguishable from the herring gull by its smaller size and thinner wings), as well as for Eleanora's falcon. Near the summit of the central hill stand the large and evocative ruins of the abandoned monastery of the Annunciation, dating from the 18th century. In common with those on Kyrá Panaghiá, Gioúra and Pipéri, the monastery was a dependency of the Grand Lavra Monastery on Mount Athos.

The open waters around Skántzoura and Pipéri are a good place to glimpse the graceful banking and swooping movements of the two kinds of shearwater which frequent the waters of the Park: the Mediterranean yelkouan shearwater, and the larger and less common Cory's shearwater, which has a wingspan of more than a metre, and is distinguished by a pure white underside with dark tailbar. There are also sightings of cetaceans in these waters: the Sperm whale, the Long-finned pilot whale, and very occasionally the Orca, or Killer whale (the largest species of the dolphin family): striped dolphin and common dolphin are also often seen.

THE MEDITERRANEAN MONK SEAL

There are probably less than 500 pairs of Mediterranean monk seal (*Monachus monachus*) surviving in the world today. Traditionally hunted for their skins and oil, and killed by fishermen who saw them as a competitor for fish stocks, their numbers have recently dwindled further as a result of disturbance and pollution resulting from the human presence along the coasts which the seals frequent. The heart of the problem is the vulnerability of the female when gestating and nursing her young. The reproduction cycle is slow and the female, if unnaturally disturbed, can easily abort. She normally gives birth to the single pup on a beach or in a cave, and will nurse it for as much as six weeks, living off accumulated fat and not fishing or eating during the entire period. After weaning, the pup may still stay with the mother for up to three years. With the arrival of industrial fishing and the increasing construction of the Mediterranean shore, the seal which once basked and even pupped on open beaches, has now been forced to take refuge in hidden and inaccessible caves. Occasionally, due to bad weather, a pup may become irretrievably separated from the mother. Three such cases have been found, nurtured at the Seal Rescue Centre in Steni Vala, and subsequently released into their natural environment. Their names were Theodoros, Stelios and Efstratia, and their individual characters as distinct as their names.

The seal is glimpsed basking in the *Odyssey*, and makes an occasional appearance on early Greek vases. Its was probably widely present in the whole of the Mediterranean and Black Sea littoral in Antiquity. Although it was more systematically hunted in Roman times and may have suffered a sharp decline in numbers as a result, the effect was never sufficient to endanger the survival of the species. Today, however, the seal is confined to two principal colonies: the northwest Aegean, and the Atlantic coast of Mauritania and Madeira. The mature animals may travel far in pursuit of food. They are very occasionally sighted in the Dodecanese (Karpathos, Tilos and Rhodes) and elsewhere in the Aegean.

During excavations in 1999 in the area of the

Commercial Harbour of Rhodes, a grave dating from the 1st century BC was found containing the skeleton of a monk seal, buried with funerary honours in a family inhumation, together with the remains of humans, a dog and some small grave gifts—just as if the seal had been a family member. The remarkable finds are displayed in the Rhodes Aquarium Museum. Fascinating in what this tells us about attitudes to animals in Antiquity, it also underlines the intelligence and potential for sociability of the seal. Ironically its trusting nature has tended only to contribute to its extinction. It has left it barely surviving as one of the world's rarest mammals.

PRACTICAL INFORMATION

370 05 **Alonnisos** (sometimes written Alónissos), also referred to by its Mediaeval name 'Chelidromi(a)' (and a current local variant, 'Liadromia'): area 65sq. km; perimeter 81km; resident population 2399; max. altitude 475 m. **Port Authority**: T. 24240 65595. **Travel information** both for Alonnisos and for visits to the outlying islands: Ikos Travel (T. 24240 65320, fax 65321, www.ikostravel.com)

ACCESS

By boat: There is no direct ferry route from Athens to Alonnisos. Services are from Volos or Aghios Konstantinos (closer to Athens): by car ferry (6 hours) daily from Volos, and five times weekly from Aghios Konstantinos. The island is also connected by rapid hydrofoil service (*Flying Dolphin*) in 2 hrs 30 mins from both of the above ports with varying frequency throughout the year. All services to the island stop in Skiathos and Skopelos en route. In the summer months, the hydrofoil connection is more frequent and the network extends to include Thessaloniki to the north and Kymi and other destinations on Euboea to the south. Access to the outlying islands in the Marine Park (with the exception of Pipéri which is closed to ordinary visits) can be arranged with a boat operator in Patitíri: there are boats of varying size—the *M/V 'Gorgona'* (Ikos Travel, details above); *'Plantiri'* (Alonnisos Travel, T. 24240 65188); and the smaller *'Stella'*.

LODGING

Chora is a cooler, quieter and more panoramic place to stay than the port: **Fantasia House** (*T. 24240 65186*), to the left as you approach the village, is attractive and simple. In Patitíri, the **Hotel Haravgi** (*T. 24240 65090, fax 65189*) is comfortable and pleasant, and open most of the year. There are many room- or studio-rental solutions on the island, which can be found at www.alonissos.gr.

EATING

A good place to sample the island's traditional, spiral *tyropitta* called *'striphtikó'* is at the taverna **'To Paradosiakó'** at Steni Vala where they are freshly and delicately made along with a variety of good fish dishes, and where fresh wine from the island is served in the late spring.

FURTHER READING

Άνω Μαγνήτον Νησοὶ, Kostas Mavrikis, Alonnisos 1997 (currently only in Greek), is a comprehensive historical study of the island and its waters. Walking on Alonnisos is a popular pastime. The following knowledgeable and informative guide can be of help: *Alonnisos Through the Souls of your Feet*, Chris Browne, 2008 (available through www.alonnisoswalks. co.uk). For information on the North Sporades Marine Park, see: www.alonissos-park.gr

SKYROS

There is a tenacity to tradition on Skyros which comes of the island being genuinely more isolated than most. It affects all aspects of life—local song and music, the decorating of houses, the breeding of horses, the preparing of cheese, the nature of festivals—and the islanders take an unostentatious pride in it. It is still possible to see sandals that would have been familiar to Theocritus on the feet of goatherds on Skyros today, or to watch carnival dances that might have come straight from a comedy of Aristophanes. The mainland feels a long way away here because the great wall of the mountains of Euboea literally and metaphorically blocks the island's view of the rest of the world. Skyros is large (more than 200sq. km) and the inhabitants are few (2,700); for this reason it feels quiet, spacious and self-contained.

Its geography is that of virtually two different islands: the north—fertile and densely wooded, scattered with habitation and cultivation—is like the other islands of the Northern Sporades: the south—empty, mountainous, wild and rocky—has more the landscape of a Cycladic island. Sophocles called the island 'windy'; Statius called it 'rocky'; Pindar and Strabo praised its herds of goat; and

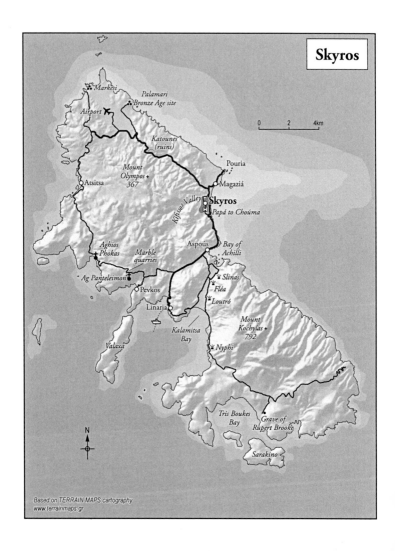

Skyros

0   2   4km

Markesi
Palamari
Bronze Age site
Airport
Katounes
(ruins)
Pouria
Mount
Olympos 367
Magaziá
Atsitsa
Kifisós Valley
Skyros
Papá to Choúma
Aghios
Phokas
Marble
quarries
Aspoús
Bay of
Achilli
Ag Panteleimon
Slinas
Fléa
Pevkos
Loutró
Linariá
Mount
Kochylas
792
Kalamitsa
Bay
Nyphi
Valaxá
N
Tris Boukes
Bay
Grave of
Rupert Brooke
Sarakino

Based on TERRAIN MAPS cartography
www.terrainmaps.gr

the tyrant Polycrates of Samos is said to have appreciated the quality of its meat. All these attributes are as true today as they were over two thousand years ago.

Matching the variety of landscape is a wonderful diversity of things of interest for the visitor to Skyros. A breed of wild horse—more pony—which is ancient and unique to the island; the quarries of a flamboyantly coloured marble, exported in large quantities to Rome in Imperial times; the moving and solitary grave of the young poet Rupert Brooke, who died at sea off Skyros at the outset of the First World War and was hurriedly buried in an olive grove above the bay of Tris Boukes. At Palamari is one of the most important and impressive Bronze Age sites in the Aegean, its ramparts and bastions clearly visible again more than 4,000 years after their construction. The island's beautiful Chora is also rich in a wide range of history: its acropolis, inhabited in prehistoric times, has walls and towers from Classical antiquity; on its summit are the impressive ruins of a 9th century episcopal church and a 15th century Venetian castle; and below is an area of interesting and beautiful streets, with painted and decorated churches and houses of a very particular, traditional architecture. All this is complemented by two small museums which do ample justice to both the island's ancient and recent history.

From cliffs and dramatic heights, to gentle bays forested with pines, from quiet springs to squares thronged with local life, Skyros lacks little to reflect the changing moods and needs of the traveller's spirit.

HISTORY AND LEGEND

Achilles sojourned on the island: disguised as a girl, he was sent by his mother Thetis to the court of Lycomedes, king of Skyros, to prevent his going to the Trojan War. Her precaution was in vain: by a subtle ploy, Odysseus uncovered the disguise and lured the hero to Troy, where he was eventually killed before the city fell. Neoptolemos, or Pyrrhos ('red-head'), son of Achilles and Deidameia, daughter of Lycomedes, grew up in Skyros, and was also taken to the Trojan War by Odysseus after his father's death (Sophocles, *Philoctetes*, 239). It was in Skyros that Lycomedes treacherously killed Theseus, king of Athens, who had sought asylum with him, by pushing him 'over a high cliff' (Plutarch, *Theseus*, 35).

There are important Neolithic and Bronze Age sites on Skyros, with clear trading links to the Northern Aegean and the Troad. The most important and best understood is Palamari, which was a flourishing centre in the late 3rd millennium BC. Apart from a (probably fortuitous) lacuna of evidence for settlement between 1650 and 1300 BC—the time of the heroes, Theseus and Achilles—there appears to have been significant habitation uninterruptedly through to the Geometric period, and into Archaic and Classical times. In 476/5 BC Cimon of Athens came to Skyros, conquered the island, enslaved the inhabitants and planted Athenian settlers (Thucydides I, 98). An augury led him to where the bones of Theseus were buried; he had them disinterred, transported them to Athens and there buried them in state in a Heröon near to the Acropolis—thought by some to be what we call the Theseion today. Skyros thereafter remained an Athenian clerurchy, with only brief interruptions—when it was ceded to Sparta between 404 and 394 BC, at the end of the Peloponnesian War, and again when it was held by the Macedonians between 322 and 197 BC. It was captured by the Roman fleet in 197 BC, but was only finally taken for Rome by Sulla in 86 BC.

Invading Goths pillaged the island in 276 AD, and the Saracen Arabs during the 9th century. In the 4th century, Skyros was promoted to a bishopric; in 895 the Episkopi church was built, and in 960 the church of St George founded on the Kastro. After the Fourth Crusade of 1204, Skyros came under Frankish domination, but was returned to Greek Byzantine control in 1276. Less than a century later, in 1354, it was taken by Giovanni Sanudo V, Duke of Naxos, and a systematic repair of the citadel's walls was undertaken by the new overlords. After the capture of Constantinople it was ceded in 1453 by Sultan Mehmet II to the Venetians, who held it for 85 years. In 1538, the Turkish admiral, Khaireddin Barbarossa, captured the island and returned it to a subsequent three centuries of Turkish dominance, with only a brief interlude between 1770 and 1774 during the Russo-Turkish War, when the island was temporarily occupied by Russian forces. Skyros participated in the Greek Independence uprising in 1821 and became part of the new Greek State, together with the other Sporades islands, in 1830.

The guide to the island has been divided into two sections:
* *Skyros Chora and environs*
* *Around the island*

SKYROS CHORA & ENVIRONS

CHORA

The steep and dramatic site of ***Skyros Chora and its acropolis** is a gift of nature for any settlers seeking a safe refuge for their dwellings which could be easily defended. The fame of its form had even reached Homer who refers to it in the *Iliad* (IX, 666-668) as 'αἰπύς' (steep). The palace of Lycomedes, where Achilles was hidden, must have been here, for whoever was 'king' of this castle was lord of the island of Skyros, and whoever was lord of Skyros chose this place to be the expression of that dominance. When the 9th century bishop of Skyros, 2,000 years after Lycomedes, sat enthroned in the middle of his clerics at the centre of the *synthronon* in the church of the Episkopí on the very same spot, he was making his power and supremacy similarly clear to his flock.

  The busy town below the acropolis is so hidden from the seaward side and from the view of passing pirates, that you could sail up and down the east coast of the island and hardly know that it existed. Before the few houses and buildings which have been erected in the last 100 years appeared on the eastern slope, there was nothing

to give away the presence of the Chora. For much of the
history of the Aegean, coastal communities have been so
constantly a prey to piracy and the power of princes or
prelates so vulnerable to attack and contestation, that it
was of the utmost importance to build on sites as hidden
and as impregnable as this.

In addition to its natural defences, the acropolis was
heavily fortified and re-fortified in different epochs. Most
visible today are the mid-13th century **Frankish fortifications** (restored in 1354 by Giovanni Sanudo, Duke of
Naxos) at the summit, compactly constructed in irregular
stone with no sharp angles in their course. Mainly at the
south and seaward sides, but also at other points, it is clear
that these early mediaeval fortifications are in turn built
on top of the larger rectangular ashlar masonry of the ancient late 5th century BC walls. The most visible evidence
of this enceinte is what remains of the gates and towers in
the lower walls (which were repaired and rebuilt in the 4th
century BC). These are visible on the east side of the acropolis, half way between the summit and the sea, and also at
the north end below *Plateia Brooke*. They are massively yet
precisely constructed and would have been a more effec-
tive deterrent than their later mediaeval counterparts.

A visit to the upper town of Skyros best begins at the
slightly soulless esplanade known as *Plateia Brooke*, half

way between Chora and the castle at the northern end of
the acropolis hill, accessible by road from the coastal side
or by foot from Chora. There is a good view from here
over the coastal plain of Kambos, an area dense in archaeological finds from Archaic and Geometric times, which
stretches from Magaziá northwards and which must always have been the island's food-basket. The sandstone
quarries at Pouriá are visible on the eastern point. The
plateia is open and windswept and makes the nakedness
of the **bronze statue** in memory of Rupert Brooke, which
is the focus of the area, a little uncomfortable. Rupert
Brooke was buried on Skyros after dying at sea during the
First World War (*see pp. 128–129*). In reality this is not a
statue of the poet but of the spirit of 'Immortal Poetry',
erected in 1930 in memory of Brooke. It is the work of a
notable sculptor from Andros, Michalis Tombros. It pos-
sesses the seriousness and academic qualities typical of
Tombros: even though it is the depiction of a 'spirit', there
is a certain 'earthbound-ness' to the piece, which is also
characteristic of his works.

From here a stepped street leads up towards the summit. Approximately 50m up on the left, is the church of
the **Aghii Pende Martyres** (The Five Holy Martyrs). Before the entrance door are ancient grave *loculi*, cut into
the rock underfoot: there are more inside. This was the

area of one of the ancient city's cemeteries. The church, which probably dates from the 13th century, is tiny and preserves slightly damaged remains of paintings from a later century in its upper area and in the shallow dome. Further up the street, the main path to the centre of Chora leads off down to the right. The uphill path twists to the left, and after a further 20m, rises alongside the large church of the **Panaghia**, which stands to the left. This is the principal church of the upper Chora, with an ornate unpainted wooden iconostasis. On the exterior of the church's south side, a wide decorated sandstone arch frames a window: it is 17th century work, depicting a fruit-vine which finishes in two scallop shells, and frames an eroded coat of arms in the centre. This elegant detail may have framed a water fountain here before the window was opened in the wall. A few metres to the south of the church of the Panaghia, and entered under the arch of a building, is the ancient church of **Aghios Athanasios**. A marble plaque by the entrance, placed by a certain (?Bishop) Theodoros, is of the 16th century, but the church is older. Its interior is simple, but contains a number of slender marble columns with early Byzantine capitals. There are the remains of wall-paintings, with some particularly well-preserved decorative passages with abstract designs.

On returning to the axial path leading up the hill, beside a small shaded *plateia* on the right, is the **Skyrian Town House Museum** of the Yalouris family. (*Open daily, except Mon, in July and Aug, with erratic opening times outside the summer months.*) This is a neatly preserved Skyrian dwelling, typical of houses in this part of the Chora, which are mostly earlier than the 19th century ones in the town below. It is only the size of these houses, and not the basic design, that changes with time.

THE SKYRIAN HOUSE

The Skyrian town house is based on a single (often small) volume, about as broad as it is high, and with a proportionately greater length—a 5 x 7m plan, with 3.5m height, would be typical. There is usually an '*avlí*', or small paved area, separating it from the street. The interior volume is divided vertically into two parts by an often ornately carved wooden partition called the '*boulmés*'. The front half of the house, entered from the street, which rises the whole height of the building is the reception area where hospitality to visitors is offered ('*spíti*', the Greek word for a house, is cognate with the Latin '*ospitium*' and our word 'hospitality'). Located in this front portion is the conical fire-place and, displayed on wooden shelves so as to impress visitors, are every kind of ceramic, metal and glass object which a family might possess: most prized of all were any that came from overseas. The rear half of the house behind the partition screen is further divided horizontally into a kitchen area below and a sleeping area above. The former, the '*apokrevátos*', will often have large storage jars occupying much of the space, sometimes half-interred for greater refrigeration. The sleeping area above, which in winter benefits from the warmth generated in the kitchen and the fireplace below and is reached by a steep and sometimes ornate staircase or ladder from the front room, is called the '*sófas*'—from the word for the low couches on which the whole family would sleep. Some privacy from below was afforded by a low, carved parapet about 20–30cm high.

The roofs of the houses had an insulation that maintained warmth in winter and cool in summer: above a dense raftering in bound canes supported by wooden cross-beams was an insulating layer comprising much finer canes with leaves and young branches, and a 10–15cm layer of dried seaweed.

This was bound and sealed by a dark, clayey earth called '*melangí*', which is impermeable and dries like a cement. The roof has a low parapet all round and is slightly pitched to allow water to drain into a down-pipe and be stored in cisterns to provide for the dry months of the year. The houses possessed few, or even no, windows. In such cases there is normally a double-door onto the outside—a main door and an external '*xóporto*', which was only half its height, and had a carved face and top. This, if used when the main door was open, allowed a modicum of privacy from the street, without blocking the passage of light and air from outside. Even though they possess nota-ble thermal qualities for the extreme temperatures of the year, these are houses made for a predominantly outdoor life-style and for a kind of society whose doors are, to this day, hardly ever closed.

Shortly beyond the Yalouris House, the street doubles back on itself. Opposite you as you climb up is the in-teresting 14th century church of the **Aghia Triada** (Holy Trinity). In front of it stand two antique columns—one in Euboean *cipollino* marble with sweeping striations; into the bell tower above have been set two Ottoman 16th century Iznik tiles. (*If locked, the key is held in a house to the left: lower door at no. 93.*) The interior is a simple dome on a square plan, with apse. Almost every surface is painted and decorated, although the condition of the murals is not good in places. There is a traditional icono-logical program to the lay-out: a *Christ Pantocrator* in the crown of the dome, surrounded by *Seraphim and Arch-angels*; the four *Evangelists* in the pendentives, mediat-ing between the circular heavens above and the square, earthly world below; and holy scenes from this world on the walls lower down. In front of the (much-repaired) wooden iconostasis, stand two Byzantine candlesticks, again in *cipollino* marble.

A short distance above Aghia Triada, to the left before the last right turn below the castle gate, the entrance-way of a house is paved entirely with Skyrian polychrome marble: this is at its most colourful when wet. (*See 'Skyr-ian Marble', pp. 122-124.*) The gate to the **Kastro** stands at the top of the street, surmounted by a marble lion. Although placed by the Venetians during their 85 year presence here, this is not the customary Venetian winged lion of St Mark; it is probably an ancient fragment which served as a grave marker, and for this reason has no wings. (*The Kastro was extensively damaged by an earth-quake in 1999, and the area and its buildings endangered.*

It is currently closed, but entry to parts of the area can be arranged with the agreement of the pappás *of the parish of St George, who resides at the Metropolitan Church of Aghios Giorgios, on the road north from the crossroads of Magaziá, just before the Molos/Airport road junction.*) Through the gate, you enter the tiny square below the **monastery of St George** (sometimes referred to here as 'St George the Arab' or 'St George the Skyrian'), founded in 960 under the Emperor Nicephorus Phocas. Scattered around in this small space are many ancient and Early Christian stone fragments from the Kastro area. The monastery, which is built up against the rock to the left, is entered through a covered area at a lower level. Beside the steps leading to the church is a fresco of St George in which unusual pictorial emphasis is given to the damsel in her tower whom George is saving from the dragon. The fine interior of the *catholicon* (considerably damaged and with most of its icons removed to safety) has a high dome supported on slender monolithic columns. There are extensive 16th century wall-paintings on the north wall (soldier saints, with scenes from the *Life of Christ* above) in strikingly rich colours. The finely carved **wooden iconostasis** is 18th century and incorporates some minute scenes—the *Temptation, Sacrifice of Isaac*, etc.—along the rail below the icons.

A long rising tunnel leads to a narrow staircase above a sheer drop giving onto the upper Kastro area. Directly in front of you is the large tri-apsidal east end of the **church of the Episkopí**, dedicated to the Assumption of the Virgin, founded in 895 AD and once the seat as its name implies of the Bishop of Skyros. Ninth century churches of this magnitude are not common, and this one is 100 years older than the monastery of Megali Lavra on Mount Athos, to which it now belongs and depends. The building was originally domed and extended as far as the door thresholds visible to the west: the interior was painted as vestiges of murals in the window niches show. The central apse contains the *synthronon*, or tiered seating for the clergy, with the central throne for the bishop in the middle. Here he sat in state, just as his pagan predecessors had done before him on this same summit. Higher up the hill, the huge vaulted double-chambered structure which crowns the rise to the north is a magazine erected during the Venetian occupation of the Kastro between 1453 and 1538. Nothing remains to be seen of any ancient temple or palace on the site, although finds in the area—such as the large piece of architrave with a *triglyph* displayed in the courtyard of the Archaeological Museum—are evidence of their existence.

The Museums

On returning to *Plateia Brooke*, the **Archaeological Museum** is below the square, down the steps to the east. (*Open 8.30–3; closed Mon.*) This is a small well-displayed collection whose principal importance lies in the rare artefacts it houses from the Geometric period (11th–8th centuries BC), which give life and substance to the few, unadorned archaeological sites that exist from this period.

There are a number of very early objects, going back to the 3rd and 2nd millennia BC, from both Palamari and the Kastro area. A couple of these pieces show, through a common pattern of design, trading connections with Troy during this early period: the **double-chalice** (*no. 893*), which is a type of object known much later to Homer; and the grey, pointed vase (*no. 754*) in Case 1. There is a fine, late Bronze Age **vase decorated with a shallow,** **high-prowed ship** (*no. 77*) in Case 2, which gives a fascinating glimpse of the craft that may have populated the seas in Mycenaean times. From the Geometric period are jewellery, stone artefacts, a number of very fine vases and a variety of other household items (braziers, etc.) in pottery. Especially worthy of note is the circular *****ritual object** (also of the Geometric period), found in a grave in the Magaziá area, which comprises eight ducks in a circle, with two snakes winding over them and devouring a dove. In combining symbols of the air (birds) and of the darkest earth (serpents) into an integrated arrangement of striking design, the piece shows the imaginative richness of this early world. Many designs from this period imitate woven, basket-work (*no. 172, case 7*). On other objects the perfect geometric forms are accomplished with the aid of a compass-pair, or by pin-and-string drawing: some of the pots (*e.g. no. 214, case 4*) still bear the pin-hole made at the centre of the concentric designs. The beautiful jewellery contained in the last cases is mostly of the late Geometric and early Archaic periods—the 8th and 7th centuries BC: there is a very fine round gold ornament (*no. 1025, case 9*), which has four swastika designs (sun symbols) embossed in it—three face clockwise, one anti-clockwise; and a rare 8th century *diadem in electrum**, beautifully embossed with designs of warriors and shields, found in an aristocratic grave at Choraphá, to the north of the Kastro hill. The small sculpture display from Classical times includes a sensitively carved fragment of a 5th century BC grave *stele*: unusually, it has been recarved in Roman times with a funeral banquet scene on its reverse side.

The corner room of the museum is dedicated to a reconstruction of the interior of a Skyriot town house (*see pp. 105–107*). Here the small seating-furniture is intricately carved, and the *boulmés* screen has motifs with cockerels and the double-headed eagle of Byzantium. Some exquisite embroideries and textiles are also exhibited. Below *Plateia Brooke*, 30m beyond and to the north, the street ends in a terrace above the impressive semicircular remains of the '**Palaiopyrgos**', or northern bastion of the late Classical enceinte of the acropolis. Between the two, to the east, is the **Manos Faltaïts Museum** (*open daily March–Nov 9–2, 6–8*) whose rich variety of displays should not be missed.

This is a private collection dedicated both to Skyrian traditions and artefacts, and to the life, family and paintings of Manos Faltaïts. The family was one of the island's wealthiest, and the unusual name is a 'Russian-isation', adopted by the painter's great-grandfather who worked and traded at the time in Odessa, of the family's Greek name. The lower store-rooms of this spacious house are an exhibition area for many of the artist's paintings. Manos Faltaïts had a number of whimsical stylistic qualities in common with Marc Chagall, but there are strong Byzantine overtones in his work; he mainly uses a Fauvist colour-range. The upper part of the house exhibits furniture, textiles (some exquisite **nuptial embroideries**, composed of designs with ancient symbolism), costumes, implements and wood-work, which are well presented and explained: they illustrate how the particularity of Skyrian workmanship arises from a very particular synthesis of Ottoman, Venetian and Byzantine influences. There are examples of decorated Skyrian pottery—amongst them the jugs which were left unglazed to allow water inside to remain cooler, and which were placed in baskets of thyme so as to impart a fresh odour to the water. The most memorable exhibit is perhaps the extraordinary **goat-costume**, used in the pre-Lenten festivities and dances on Skyros: this example weighs nearly 60kg.

SKYRIAN CARNIVAL GOAT DANCE

How ancient the Goat Dance may be and how much it has changed in form with time is difficult to establish, but it is a striking example of how ancient pagan practices have survived intact in isolated corners of the Greek world such as Skyros. In Antiquity the island was famed for its goats which are mentioned by Pindar (early 5th century BC), by Strabo (1st century BC) and by the philosopher-gourmand, Athenaeus of Naucratis (2nd century AD). The Goat Dance celebrates the importance that both goat and goatherd have always had on the island: a goatherd with large flocks possessed considerable wealth and a very particular status in society. During the carnival period the young men of the island dress in an all-covering costume of goat-skin hung with bells, and with a goat-head mask, and participate in a noisy dance along with other allegorical figures, such as young men who are dressed—as Achilles had been, in the court of Lycomedes—in women's clothing. The goat-figure is called the '*gerós*', from the Greek word for strong and sturdy—an attribute the young men need to posses, given that the costume can weigh as much as 60kg. On the last day of the festivities they remove the costume and dance once again, freed of its terrible weight: the symbolic significance of this gesture is appropriate to the last day of carnival, when the encumbrance of earthly needs should be set aside for the period of Lenten penitence.

The environs of Chora

The lower Chora, reached by taking the path downhill from just above the church of the Pende Martyres, stretches in a chain of tiny squares and spaces along a gracefully curving main street. In the valley below the town to the west lies the **River Kifissos**—named by the

Athenian occupants of Skyros of the 5th century BC after the river of the same name that flowed through the Attic plain in Athens. This valley soon leads out of the town to the west through olive groves and into a beautiful hilly landscape, with old stone houses and bridges. The area is pleasant for walking and there are good views back towards the town and the acropolis.

Below the south precipice of the acropolis of Kastro is the modern cemetery, and behind it to the south rises the hill of 'Fourka' (in effect an extension of the acropolis hill), named after the gallows erected here by the Turks. On the summit are the remains of the platform of the **Archaic Temple of Apollo** (6th century BC), which would have been a landmark clearly visible from the sea. The bed-rock has been cut around its podium, and the stone for the temple's construction will have come from the quarried area just to the right of the path as you climb up. The temple is oriented on a north/south axis, and was unusually broad (17.5m) in relation to its length (24m). This hill could be the 'place which had the appearance of a mound' mentioned by Plutarch as being the site of the tomb of Theseus from which Cimon took the hero's bones, returning them triumphantly to Athens in 476 BC.

The fertile plain of the Kampos which stretches to the *north* of Chora up the coast has been the scene of many archaeological finds, showing that the area had been an important place of continuous settlement and burial from pre-Mycenaean through to Hellenistic times. At its easternmost point is the fascinating landscape of the **ancient sandstone quarries** of Pouriá. The road ends by a windmill on the promontory in front of a large rectangular outcrop of stone with a white-fronted church cut into its lower right-hand corner: the simple chapel is dedicated to St Nicholas and is hewn out of the last remaining piece which has survived un-quarried from the soft *poros* stone which once constituted the whole promontory. From here to the south, the entire waterfront is cut away in regular rectangular shapes and declivities. This is a type of stone which was easy to cut and shape, and could be loaded here directly onto shallow barges for transportation.

The stretch of the coast extending an equal distance to the *south* of Chora, has also been rich in early archaeological finds: a late Mycenean cemetery at Básales; an earlier Neolithic settlement at 'Papá to Choúma' (on the coast directly south-east of the town); and even earlier Mesolithic finds in a cave in the **bay of Achilli**. According to tradition this wide bay was the point of Achilles' fateful departure for Troy. It is more than likely that there was an important altar somewhere here in Archaic and Classical times, since Achilles early on came to be worshipped as a chthonic divinity on Skyros.

AROUND THE ISLAND

(Chora = 0.0km for distances in the text)

PALAMARI AND MARKESI

North from Chora, after a succession of narrow valleys dotted with tiny chapels, the view to the northern end of the island opens out at a point where the whole hillside near the road is scattered with the deserted 18th and 19th century houses of the once large community of Katoúnes (6km). At 7.5km, a track to the right leads to the important excavations at *Palamari (8.5km). The geography of the site—treeless and sandy—on a low eminence jutting out into the sea beside a sheltered cove has many elements that are characteristic of other Aegean prehistoric settlements such as Poliochni on Lemnos or Philakopi on Milos. This is an early Bronze Age port, founded in the middle of the 3rd millennium BC and inhabited continuously until around 1650 BC, at which point it appears to have been permanently abandoned. Dominating the (metal) trade-routes of these early times could be a dangerous occupation: hence the large and remarkably well-preserved fortifications.

The sophistication of design and organisation of the settlement is impressive. There are well-designed bastions, ditches, military store-rooms directly behind the walls, and hidden corridors communicating between the bastions on the inside—all standard fare for constructions of much later centuries but a surprise to find here, so early. The ring of **walls** (on the landward side) is well preserved to a height of nearly 3m in places, and is punctuated regularly with the bases of fine **semicircular towers**. The houses which have been excavated so far lie further inside the site. They are constructed in a variety of types and colours of stone seemingly brought from different parts of the island. By comparison with those in Akrotiri on Santorini, these dwellings, separated by narrow passage-ways, can seem cramped and small, but their hearths, storage areas, doorways, stone benches and ovens are all well-constructed nonetheless. The carefully constructed **drainage channels** beneath the walls of the town are emblematic of the settlement's remarkable and sophisticated planning.

The settlement's water source has been identified in the

area of the houses. To the east a considerable part of the town has been eroded by the sea, so we may only be looking today at just over half of the original area of the settlement—a state of affairs reminiscent of Phylakopi on Milos. The rocks below the surface of the water and the erosion of the city make it difficult to reconstruct where exactly the harbour was. For a settlement with such a strategic position, controlling the crucial maritime trade-routes to Lemnos and Troy in the northeast Aegean, a functional and protected port would have been essential.

At 9.5km from Chora is a right turn for Skyros airport. Beyond this point another right turn (11.7km) leads to the ancient site of **Markési** at the northwestern tip of the island. (It lies inside an active military zone of the Greek Air Force, and is currently out of bounds unless a permit is previously obtained from the military authorities in Athens.)

The site was continually inhabited and used from the Early Bronze Age through to Christian times. The remains of an ancient settlement and of **rock-cut tombs** are in evidence on the promontory. The hill is marked by the church of the *Theotokos*; beneath this are the remains of an **Early Christian church**, which in turn is built over the base of a **Clas-**

sical temple to Poseidon. The dedication to the god of the seas is not surprising given the strategically panoramic position and the busy maritime routes it surveys—a fact which has not escaped the attention of the Hellenic Ministry of Defence.

Inland of the road an active quarry is visible which produces the grey-veined white marble of the island—a less beautiful version of Euboea's *cipollino* marble which is more elegantly veined in blue and green. From here, the road turns south through dense forests of Aleppo pine, along the west coast of the island.

THE WEST COAST

At **Atsítsa** (13km, by direct route from Chora; 18km by the above route) the road descends into a sheltered bay with a pleasant taverna and small hotel. The pale green colour in the cliff to the south signifies the presence of iron ore in the area; the remains of an early 20th century mining plant are still visible in the overhead viaduct and the stone buildings of the loading station at the shore.

South from here, the road continues through pine forests passing tranquil bays, empty beaches and beautiful views. (*The road surface is unmade, but passable for ordinary vehicles.*) After 6km, the track comes down to the shore at **Aghios Phokás** where an enormous antique block of cut stone beside the taverna on the shore declares an ancient presence in the area. On top of the low rise at the south end of the bay is the chapel of Aghios Phokás; in front of it are the remains of a much older building, the cornerstone of which is a massive well-cut monolith of the colourful brecciated marble for which Skyros was famous in Roman times. A line of large dressed blocks stretches in a north/south line in front of the church and other impressive pieces lie around: an area of the bedrock has been extensively cut in the undergrowth just to the east side. There was a monastery previously at this site, and it would seem that it had been built in turn out of these remains of an earlier, pagan construction. The eroded surface of the marble looks dull in the bright light, but a splash of water immediately brings life back to its kaleidoscopic colours.

SKYRIAN MARBLE

This is the *marmor scyrium*, beloved of the Romans for its tender and variegated colours and the fine polish it could be given. In truth, it is not one but a whole group of marbles whose subtle variations depend on where on the island and where in the quarry the stone was taken. It was later called in Italian *breccia di settebassi* (or *settebasi*) after the ancient Roman villa of Settebassi outside Rome on the Via Appia, where many examples of it were found. This was a marble whose often extreme colourfulness went to the heart of Imperial Roman decorative taste. It has a predominantly pale purple-red hue, shot through with *breccie*, or breaches, of yellow and pink and red. It appealed just as much in 17th century Rome for the decorating of the great post-Renaissance palaces in the city— by which time it was not being quarried any more in Skyros but simply being lifted from ancient Roman ruins and re-used. The Romans were refined connoisseurs of the subtleties and variations in the chromatic range of such marbles: although abundant in nature, the best qualities of Skyrian marble were always elusive. Only certain veins of the large quarries produced the small size of oblong variegations in red, pink and yellow which were most desired in the metropolis. It was the job of the quarry-master to locate these prized qualities for the market. A fine example of Skyrian marble is the massive pedestal and urn at the extreme south end of the *Galleria delle Carte Geografiche* in the Vatican Palace in Rome. It is the last object you see before you descend the stairs into the Sistine Chapel.

Several **marble quarries**—small and large, superficial and deep, ancient and modern—are to be found all around in this area. To the north of Aghios Phokás they produce a largely white marble with orange veining, but at the top of the track to the south there are those that yield the high quality, polychrome stone. The best marble appears fleetingly and unexpectedly, often amongst areas that seem very ordinary. In its natural form, it may seem unremarkable, but its decorative beauty comes out when wet or when cut and polished. The area of the quarries is protected by the presence of the church of St Panteleimon which stands beside the road, overlooking the sea. St Panteleimon's work as a healer and doctor made him a natural protector against the many injuries which befell those who worked in quarries.

From the church of Aghios Panteleímon the road descends steeply to the attractive bay of **Pevkos** (10km), which was the **ancient Roman harbour** for the loading and shipping of the marble. At the south end of the shore of the cove, the rock face has been cut away at an obtuse angle and clearly perforated in two parallel rows of deep square holes for mounting and fixing wooden posts for winching the heavy blocks into barges. The edge of the sea is littered with huge rectangular blocks of marble of all colours.

MOUNT KOCHYLAS AND THE SOUTH OF THE ISLAND

Between the reedy bays of Kalamítsa (south) and Achílli (north) stretches a thin band of alluvial land, probably once submerged, which effectively divides the island in two. Its east side is fed by numerous springs which rise under the steep, western slopes of **Mount Kochylas** (792m)—the **springs of Slínas, Fléa** and **Loutró**, the last with a rather poor-tasting water. From here the road hugs the west shore of the Kochylas massif and after the church of the Aghia Triada at Nyphi, climbs up onto an open and mountainous plateau—the domain of goats and of a sparse *maquis* which they keep assiduously cropped. These wild slopes are also the winter domain of the Skyrian horse, a diminutive and ancient breed, traditionally used on the island as a packhorse.

THE SKYRIAN HORSE

In the central and southern valleys of the island, it is common to see the wild Skyrian horse grazing freely. Though 'wild' in the sense of freely roaming, its temperament is notably placid. Never more than 1–1.1m in (shoulder) height, this is a rare and distinct species of horse which is known from as early as Mycenaean times and may have changed little from its ancient ancestors. At the beginning of the 2nd millennium BC a nomadic people entered Greek lands from the central Eurasian steppe-lands: we know little about them except that they were good potters and that they came with horses. Those horses may well have been of a form similar to the ones that now graze on Skyros, whose size and nature—because of their isolation—has not evolved or been modified through the cross-breeding, principally with Berber stock, which has characterised commoner breeds. If not already present from before, the horses may first have been introduced onto the island by Athenian colonists in the course of the 7th and 6th centuries BC. In fact the horses pictured in the Parthenon frieze appear very small by comparison with their modern counterparts and may have been of a similar kind to those on Skyros today. The horses winter in the wilder southern half of the island and then migrate to the northern part in search of greenery and shade during the hotter months. Their number on the island is fewer than 150 with few examples elsewhere, and there are naturally concerns for their survival as a breed.

The northern branch of the road (junction at 19km) continues high above the wide sweep of the bays below, and leads, after a long descent by switchbacks, to the wild and deserted cliff-scenery of the island's southeast corner (26km). The southern branch of the road, descends to **Tris Boukes Bay** (or 'Tre Bocche')—its name referring to the three entrances into the bay defined by the two islands of Plateía and Sarakinó, just off-shore. With the presence of more ancient quarries in the mountains inland of here, the bay of Tris Boukes was, like Pevkos, used for the shipping of stone by the Romans, who built an aqueduct in order to bring fresh water to the area. There is currently a Greek Naval installation here, and the area is inaccessible from the land road.

A little more than 100m before the entrance to the naval base, in a grove of olive trees just below the road, is the solitary **grave of Rupert Brooke** (20km). The young English poet (1887–1915), commissioned into the navy in the First World War, was buried here during the night of the 23 April 1915, having died of septicaemia the same afternoon aboard a French hospital ship, the *Duguay Trouin*. The expeditionary force, of which he was a member, sailed the following morning for the Dardanelles.

Brooke's valediction in *The Times* was written by none less than the First Lord of the Admiralty at the time, Winston Churchill: he described Brooke as 'joyous, fearless, versatile, deeply instructed, [and] with classic symmetry of mind and body'. At the time of his premature death, his personality and writing had already begun to make a considerable mark. His striking stature and good looks, with a mane of golden-red hair, caught the attention of many—amongst them, Henry James who encountered Brooke on a visit to Cambridge in 1909. His circle of friends and acquaintances included E.M. Forster, Virginia Woolf, Geoffrey and Maynard Keynes, Frances Cornford, and the Prime Minister's vivacious daughter, Violet Asquith. He travelled extensively in Europe and the United States, and then across the South Pacific to New Zealand. He stayed a while in Tahiti, where it seems that he may have fathered a child by a woman of the island. He was only 27 when his battalion set out for the Aegean in the winter of 1915. Frances Cornford, with her keen and compassionate sense of irony, later wrote of Brooke as 'A young Apollo, golden-haired … dreaming on the verge of strife/ Magnificently unprepared/ For the long littleness of life'.

The first grave here was an improvised pile of stones with two wooden crosses, but there is now a simple stone sarcophagus, with carved oak-leaves and rose decorating the cross at its head. At its foot is inscribed Brooke's famous sonnet, *The Soldier*, written in 1914. There is poignant irony in the prophetic words of the poem and its emphasis on the ultimate solitude of human existence. There are few graves more dramatically solitary than this, and few landscapes that could have been more distant from Brooke's beloved fen-lands. The remoteness of the setting and the peaceful animals grazing here, constitute in the memory one of the most indelible images of the island.

PRACTICAL INFORMATION

340 07 **Skyros**: area 208sq. km; perimeter 134 km; resident population 2711; max. altitude 792 m. **Port Authority**: T. 22220 93475. **Tourist information**: www.inskyros.gr

ACCESS

By boat: Access to the island is from the Euboean port of Kymi by daily car-ferry services (*Skyros Line*, T. 22220 22020 (Kymi) & T. 91789/91790 (Skyros)), leaving Kymi in the late afternoon and returning in the early morning (2 hrs). Less frequent (generally twice-weekly) services also operate between Skyros and the other Northern Sporades Islands, and Aghios Kostantinos on the mainland. All boats dock at the port of Linariá on the west coast, 9km from Skyros Chora.

By air: Olympic Air currently operates a 35 minute, non-stop flight to and from Athens, twice weekly on Wednesday and Saturday afternoons. The Airport is 10km north of Chora.

LODGING

The building of the former Xenia Hotel on the waterfront at Magaziá—the peaceful area just below and north of the Kastro—has re-opened as the luxurious **Hydroussa Skyros Hotel** (*T. 22220 91209 & 92063–5, fax 92062, www.hydroussahotel.gr/ skyros*), providing the island's most comfortable accommodations. Also in Magaziá, simple rooms and kindly hospitality can be found at the **Hotel Deidameia** (*T. 22220 92008; fax. 92009*); and on the coast road, right under the Kastro is the panoramic **Hotel Paliopirgos** (*T. 22220 91014 & 92185*). Both are inexpensive alternatives.

EATING

In the upper part of the main street of Chora, just as it begins to climb steeply, the **Mezedopoleion 'O Pappous'** has excellent local specialties (hot and cold), as well as a variety of Skyrian cheeses. It is popular and always full of locals and visitors alike. In Gyrismata Bay, **Stelios** fish taverna has good quality, fresh seafood.

INDEX

Nigel McGilchrist is an art historian who has lived in the Mediterranean—Italy, Greece and Turkey—for over 30 years, working for a period for the Italian Ministry of Arts and then for six years as Director of the Anglo-Italian Institute in Rome. He has taught at the University of Rome, for the University of Massachusetts, and was for seven years Dean of European Studies for a consortium of American universities. He lectures widely in art and archaeology at museums and institutions in Europe and the United States, and lives near Orvieto.